My Secret Life
on the McJob

My Secret Life
on the McJob

Lessons from
Behind the Counter
Guaranteed to Supersize
Any Management Style

Jerry M. Newman

McGraw-Hill

New York   Chicago   San Francisco
Lisbon   London   Madrid   Mexico City   Milan
New Delhi   San Juan   Seoul   Singapore
Sydney   Toronto

The *McGraw·Hill* Companies

1 2 3 4 5 6 7 8 9 0   DOC/DOC   0 9 8 7 6

ISBN 10: 0-07-147365-3
ISBN 13: 978-0-07-147365-1

Interior design by Lee Fukui and Mauna Eichner

McGraw-Hill books are available at special quantity discounts to use as
premiums and sales promotions, or for use in corporate training
programs. For more information, please write to the Director of Special
Sales, Professional Publishing, McGraw-Hill, Two Penn Plaza, New
York, NY 10121-2298. Or contact your local bookstore.

This book is printed on acid-free paper.

Contents

Acknowledgments

My seven fast food jobs led to three herniated discs. Thanks to Terrie, Erinn, and Kelly for not saying "I told you so."

Thanks to Bob Black at Kimberly-Clark for the insights that helped guide this book.

To the seven store managers who endured my ineptitude, forgive me!

Thank you, Dean John Thomas and SUNY Buffalo, for giving me time off to work in the fast food industry.

Finally, thanks to the McGraw-Hill team and to Neil Levine who helped make this book possible.

Introduction: Would You Like Fries with That Condom?

Why would a distinguished management professor ever contemplate working undercover in a string of fast food eateries? I wish I could give you a single, concrete answer to that question. But there is no one moment of epiphany to explain why I spent 14 months doing just that. I can tell you that the reasons behind this unusual journey began long before I first donned my Arby's cap and extra-tight shirt in December 2003.

Infiltrating the fast food world grew out of a single question: "What goes *on* here?!" This is a question I'm sure many fast food patrons find themselves asking on a regular basis—and probably for the same reasons I did when a breakfast run with my daughter back in early 1998 went terribly wrong. Now, I'm sure there have been countless individuals who have had experiences similar to mine, and they didn't choose to embark on a life-altering, one-person mission. They weren't driven to uncover how this industry survives and even thrives despite a host of challenges ranging from shifting consumer trends, to commoditized products, to rapid turnover. No, they didn't take 14 months out of their lives to travel around the country to the extreme annoyance of their significant others—they let the incident *go*. This brings me to the second underlying cause for my actions. I'm an academic, and the very same proclivities—I'm highly inquisitive and need to get to the reasons behind general assumptions—that serve me so well as a professor drove me on my quest.

In this book, you're going to get *me* at full throttle (you've been warned), so let's begin with a personal assessment. Working in the academic arena for as long as I have, it's natural for me to seek scientific explanations for everyday phenomena. For better or worse, as a management professor who specializes in compensation and other human resources issues, I am constantly ferreting out the reasons behind and solutions for issues that frustrate managers every day, from leadership to operations to customer satisfaction. With these character traits firmly in place and having taken root over the course of decades, I was almost driven to understand just what goes on in fast food after a defining experience transformed me from a mild-mannered, though sometimes trying, university professor into a secret agent, undercover employee working behind fast food counters in seven restaurants spread across the Midwest, East, and South.

Now that you have a sense of my own personal makeup,

let me describe the experience I shared with my daughter, Kelly, which since its occurrence in March 1998 has gone down in the annals of Newman-family lore.

As with all teenagers, Kelly found her daughterly manners when she turned 17 and yearned for a driver's license. I'd like to say that she had come to the end of a "phase" when she asked for my help in getting her learner's permit, but that was not the case: It was the call of the open road that prompted Kelly to ask for my assistance in her quest for that teenage Holy Grail. That's how we happened to be out on a cold March morning, inching our way over snowy Buffalo, New York, streets.

Thinking to avoid traffic, I suggested an early start on a sunless Sunday. Reluctantly, Kelly agreed to get started at 6:30 a.m. And, naturally, my logic prevailed: Learning with no diversions like behemoth 18 wheelers and geriatric grandmas made sense to her. If we survived (I actually think I said "When we're finished!"), I agreed to a little breakfast at one of the local fast food chains to celebrate her first driving experience.

I'll skip the driving stories. I'm alive to write this, so nothing too serious could have happened—at least until we sat down at a table in the fast food restaurant. Kelly is a finicky eater. How that's possible in a fast food restaurant I don't know, but she likes to inspect and rearrange what she eats before diving in. Me? Not so much. My breakfast sandwich was good. I like bacon, egg, and cheese sandwiches. My joy was short-lived. I heard Kelly screech, "OH MY GOD—WHAT IS THIS?" Not even daring to touch it, she showed me an open sandwich with what looked to me like the tip of a condom sticking out between the egg and the bacon.

Now, I don't typically think of myself as the overprotective fatherly type, but this sight instantly outraged me. I'm not sure what made me madder: a foreign object that was moments away from being eaten by my baby or the prospect of my having to explain what a condom was and speculating about how that condom got in the sandwich in the first place.

Maybe today, as an experienced fast food worker, I would recognize the condom as part of a rubber or plastic glove. Maybe today, I would see that it was the sliced-off tip of an index finger of that glove. At that moment, though, I thought it was a condom. A red condom to be precise because that was the color I was seeing as I barged to the front of the line at the food counter. "Where's the manager?!" I bellowed. Seeing my face and hearing the tone of my voice (I'm six feet four inches tall and a big guy—sometimes the big bear bites!), the counter worker wisely chose to summon the manager. As the supervisor approached, I unknowingly channeled the voice of professorial authority. My family says that they don't know how to define it, but they would tell you that it sounds a little like Beaver Cleaver's dad on steroids—loud, authoritative, and willing to challenge any opposition.

Holding the sandwich aloft, the unknown object dangling

obscenely over the side, I said, "My daughter found this condom in her sandwich. Do you want to explain to me how this could possibly happen? And what are you going to do to ensure it never happens again?"

By this time I had the attention of everyone waiting to order breakfast, everyone waiting to receive their breakfast, and everyone behind the counter who should have been handling the orders and distribution. For the price of a sandwich on a cold Buffalo Sunday morning, the whole group was getting a tragic comedy in one act.

Looking at the sandwich, the manager said, "Sir, that appears to be a piece of sanitary glove, not a condom." "Well, maybe that's what it is," I continued, undaunted by the correction, "but can you imagine my daughter's face when she bit into this and found what we thought was a condom?" (And actually it was still of concern that this inedible object was included in my daughter's sandwich. Refuse is refuse, after all.) The manager's face visibly moved up one notch of concern. I think the hamburger colleges across the nation must be teaching managers how to cool the mark off. "I'm sorry, sir, I don't know how this happened, but I will gladly refund your money for the sandwich." This minimal response only angered me even more. What was going *on* here?!!! There was no intense inquisition of his employees, no sleuthing to look for the glove with only four and a half fingers, no comp of the whole meal and maybe a few coupons for future meals gratis. Ballistic by this point (to the embarrassment, no doubt, of Kelly), I launched back into verbal assault mode, "So that's it? Because of incompetence or worse—sick pranksters—my daughter has a picture frozen in her brain that will probably never leave her."

The manager notched up to concern level 4, skipping 3: "Would you like to fill out a complaint form, sir?" By now I suspect that talking to the early morning shift manager on a Sunday is not likely to be my best course of action. I asked for the name and phone number of the district manager: "Maybe it is time to go to your boss. I don't feel this incident is being treated with the seriousness it deserves." In retrospect, this sounded pompous. But I'm a professor at a research university, and that's what we do when we don't know how else to make a point.

On Monday I called the district manager and described the events with, I'm afraid, a bit less of the righteous indignation I had mustered the day before. While he promised to look into the situation, it sounded more like "manager speak" than an actual call to action. I wondered at the time if this was a regular scenario. Recent events at a Wendy's in Riverside, California, suggested that even stranger finger follies are possible; remember that customer who falsely claimed to find part of a finger in her chili?

In retrospect—particularly now that I know what goes on behind the counters of fast food stores—perhaps I should have considered my daughter lucky that it was only the glove tip she discovered in her sandwich. In any event, at that time, the district manager was only mildly interested in my story, offering somewhat unconvincingly to investigate the incident, plus graciously to give me one month of free sandwiches. This was his suggested solution? I found his offer humorous in its irony. "So we find a condom in our food, and your solution is to offer me more food?" Hearing the sarcasm in my voice—note to self: sarcasm is not a good negotiating strategy—he replied, "Well, sir, again I'm sorry. And we will investigate. And we are offering you a month's worth of sandwiches. I'm not sure what else we can do for you." This is administrativese for "Get lost, this is as good as it's going to get." As a last desperate attempt to inflict a small cost on this billion-burger-a-year corporation, my final parting words were these: "Well, I guess you know this means my family will never eat at your restaurant again!" Our acting on that threat lasted about six weeks, and the restaurant seemed to survive just fine during the hiatus.

※　　※　　※

Yet, for all of its visible flaws, spending time in this world of fast food restaurants proved to me that the industry often produces good workers, strong managers, and future leaders. How did they get there? What went on behind the counter? Were glove-cutting pranks the norm? What is it about fast food restaurant policies and practices that would spur such sick behavior? In the course of 14 months, even though I didn't find the answer to the last question, I did become a fast food restaurant convert.

※　　※　　※

In the next chapter, I'll explain in detail just how I was able to get hired at not just one but seven restaurants. I'll tell you now that I did have a bit of help in the form of life experience, so I wasn't as much of a newbie as many of my fellow crew members. During my daughter's later teenage years, I began a long stint as volunteer supervisor of a concession stand for Aunt Rosie's Fastpitch Softball Tournaments. Aunt Rosie's runs the largest girls' tournaments in the Northeast, with summer weekends almost always attracting several hundred girls, parents, and fans—many of whom descended on our concession stand after games ended. For the first few years we cooked only hot dogs and hamburgers. Limited menus made lunch rush relatively easy. Over time, though, I expanded the menu, and as the menu lengthened, so did the lines. As both the cook and the supervisor, I found the job a lot less fun with customers yelling at me for delayed orders, incorrect orders, or poorly cooked food. As my small concession stand became more like fast food restaurants, my curiosity about those restaurants grew even more intense.

So now you see how a number of factors influenced my interest in learning more about the fast food restaurant business. Then opportunity turned my musings into reality. One of the pertinent things about my university job is that I focus on issues facing modern managers particularly as they relate to hiring, retaining, and compensating workers. So in the fall of 2003, I applied for a sabbatical to research management trends in fast food restaurants. My hypothesis was that the fast food industry is a pioneer in managing when cost control is imperative. In my research, I would focus on those management practices that were found to be both cost-effective for the business and beneficial to the employees and determine if it was possible to apply these findings generally to other businesses to improve productivity, keep turnover down, and control labor costs. In a nutshell, I yearned to understand how management practices are altered when margins are low and cost control becomes the most critical element in sustaining a business.

I believe my findings are valuable, although ironically not in an academic sense but as a string of astute man-on-the-street observations. The following chapters detail my story, full of hard-knock experiences in what it takes to be successful in a cost-conscious business—as both an employee and a manager.

The Rules
of the Game

A s a professor, I was methodical in how I approached this project. I decided to work at only fast food restaurants. That was the scene that had first sparked my curiosity, and it is the category within the hospitality industry that seems to generate the most interest and controversy. Having made this decision, I still needed to narrow down the criteria on which I would base my research. It wasn't easy to set those criteria because I needed to consider the practicalities of my project. Mine wasn't a university-sanctioned project funded by gobs of grant money. It was just me, on my own, making the most of the opportunity while trying to fit the effort into my existing life situation. Standard investigatory rules balanced by reality led me to select the following criteria for the project, the reasons for which I'll explain further on in this chapter. But for now, here are the rules I established for myself:

1. *Where's the beef?* I would work in stores that primarily sold burgers.

2. *I am a fugitive from a chain gang.* I would target chains, not mom-and-pop stores.

3. *I'm nationwide.* I would apply for jobs in locations where I would have a believable primary residence, which ended up being in the East, Midwest, and South. This way I would be able to dig into some cultural differences as well.

4. *Build it and they will come.* I wouldn't narrow my applications to stores that advertised job openings; I would call and inquire at restaurants that fit my other criteria.

5. *Spread the wealth around.* I wouldn't work for stores that operated under the same franchiser.

6. *Compare and contrast.* I would work in two stores operated by the same corporation.

Now for the reasons behind these very carefully selected criteria. Having narrowed my environment to fast food, I still needed to decide *which* restaurants. Initially I considered selecting one from each category of cuisine (such as pizza, chicken, or Mexican food). But I ultimately narrowed it down to places that primarily focused on beef, specifically hamburgers. My interest was in the people behind the counter, and I conjectured that by working in restaurants that had a narrow product line, I could see "people differences" that were caused by something other than "product differences." It's similar to why behavioral psychologists study identical twins raised in different homes: They hold as much constant as possible (the genetic background) so

FROM BEHIND THE COUNTER

Working in the large chains, perhaps I could put to rest the mystery of how the plastic fingertip got into my daughter's sandwich. But, alas, in the course of working on this project, I could not find a logical explanation. Crew members wear the ill-fitting gloves while handling meat—most sanitation laws require it. But I'm still at a loss to explain how the tip of a finger to one glove would end up being cut off in the course of normal operating procedures. And how a glove tip could have migrated to a sandwich is an even bigger mystery.

that whatever differences appear are likely to be caused by what's left over (different environments). Anyway, that was my thinking, and I stuck with it.

Once I settled on fast food places that sold beef, I then had to decide whether I'd go with big chains or little mom-and-pop operations. I've always been intrigued by big chains. I've eaten in them since childhood. Most people have frequented some large chain at one time or another, so if I could explain operations and describe how people behaved behind the counter of a Wendy's or a Burger King, I felt the results would hold more meaning. Ultimately, I selected McDonald's, Burger King, Wendy's, Arby's, and Krystal, which is a large chain in the Southeast that is modeled very similarly to White Castle. Originally I didn't think at all about the type of ownership structure—corporate or franchise. The vast majority of stores are owned by franchisers, and my sample closely modeled this reality. Six of the seven restaurants within the five chains noted above were franchise-owned. The seventh, a McDonald's, was corporate-owned.

My primary reason for exploring the distinction between franchise and corporate-owned stores? The leash is much shorter in corporate stores. For instance, the store manager who hired me into the corporate McDonald's apologized several times during the interview about the lack of discretion she had and that my starting salary was constrained by corporate—the first offer was $5.15 per hour, more than a dollar less than other stores in the area. She said that when the store had been a franchise only months earlier, the wages the store had paid were actually above the local competition.

※   ※   ※

It was tempting to apply only at stores right around where I lived. For one thing, job applications all call for an address. I didn't want to raise unnecessary red flags by applying at a store in Biloxi, Mississippi, for example, and giving them a New York address. But I also didn't want my research to be applicable only to New York. As much as I love Buffalo, most of the rest of the country looks on us as relevant for only two things: snow and chicken wings. To give this project a more national flavor, I decided to sample some stores in other parts of the country. Where, though? I was reluctant to go somewhere, check into a motel, and give that address as my home base on employment applications. Wouldn't a manager look suspiciously at anyone who listed under address: Sleepy Hollow Motel, Room 23? Rather than chance it, I decided to operate out of two states where I could honestly list permanent addresses.

My family has a second home in northern Florida, so I thought I might learn a little about the differences between North and South. Two of those differences became readily apparent almost immediately: cultural courtesy and labor laws. In the South, courtesy—at least on the surface—was much more evident. Anyone over 30 was addressed formally, almost to the point of being stilted. I was "Mr. Jerry." The South's labor laws intrigued me since in my day job I teach some of the more prescient national labor laws to eager young MBA students. Admittedly, though, I don't know much about state laws. New York has rules on everything. I couldn't clock in before 11 a.m. at Arby's, so said the manager. Why? State law specified a mandatory paid rest break in the first three hours for those beginning before 11 a.m. Clock in at 11, though, and the break was greatly postponed. In the South, the rules were much less restrictive. This, of course, left you to the whims of your manager. At Krystal, a jovial James made sure we got regular breaks—an unheard of half-hour. Just down the street, though, my angry Wendy's boss rationed out breaks as rewards and punishments. Didn't do

FROM BEHIND THE COUNTER

It feels strange being addressed as "Mr. Jerry," especially when it's linked to a criticism: "Now, Mr. Jerry, if you drop a tray of Angus Burgers on the floor, that will cost us more than your day's wages." It's tough being criticized and diminished all in the same "Mr. Jerry" breath! Others are also addressed more formally. The 70-something cashier is unfailingly called "Miss Judy." The salad assembler is "Miss Martha." The "Misses" and "Misters" all have a common characteristic—grey hair.

things how, when, and as quickly as he wanted? Be prepared to reside at the rear of an endless queue of crew members waiting to get a minute breather. My other state was Michigan, where I could give my sister's house as my address. Michigan is only spitting distance from Buffalo, so I didn't notice nearly the number of differences caused by culture or by enacted laws.

My choice of stores also was governed by job availability. Initially I was interested in checking for age discrimination. Because it was a physically demanding job, would I find some employers shying away from hiring more senior applicants? I felt that I could make a better case, yea or nay, for age discrimination if I applied only at places with advertised openings. Deny me employment at places with no openings and I can't begin to suspect ageism. But do the same thing at places claiming to have positions available, and maybe it's not indisputable evidence of discrimination, but if I saw a pattern of denials, I would begin to wonder.

So my first round of applications went only to stores with "Now Hiring" advertised on the marquee signs usually located at road's edge. Most of these signs were posted alternately with other signs announcing that week's special ("Angus and 'shroom burgers") and announcing "Help Wanted." One sign outside a Florida Burger King, though, sent an entirely unexpected message. On one side, in large, bold letters, was the message: "Don't put a question mark where God put a period." And on the reverse side: "Everlasting, unconditional, never failing love, God's love." I wasn't surprised to see this sign in the South, where there is much more visible evidence of religious convictions. I was surprised, though, that this message appeared on the sign for a nationwide burger chain.

Not all stores advertised openings on the marquee signs. I began to see "Now Hiring" signs in store windows and on the front counters inside the stores. In the South, it wasn't uncommon to see multiple signs on the path followed by drive-thru customers, almost like the old Burma Shave commercials populating the roadside in my youth. A row of signs that in sum make a memorable recruitment pitch: "Feeling Low?" . . . "Need Some Dough?" . . . "Got a Ride?" . . . "Apply Inside!" On occasion, when none of these outlets indicated openings, I sometimes resorted to calling selected stores that fit my other criteria, just to see if openings might exist. In Michigan, every store I called responded to my inquiry with a resounding "YES, jobs are available!" Not a single one, though, advertised on the outside.

Every store to which I applied had some evidence of available openings. Had I experienced prolonged joblessness, I might have been tempted to suspect age discrimination. I'm pleased to report, though, that I saw no evidence of this. Indeed, hiring practices seemed to be remarkably free of any evidence that certain groups were excluded.

* * *

My last two rules were not to work for multiple stores

under the same franchiser and to work for at least two stores owned by the same corporation. While I avoided applying at multiple stores under the same franchiser, early in the project, I might have inadvertently violated this rule. There is a tendency, perhaps reinforced by corporate leanings, to have the same franchiser control all stores in a given geographic area. How was I to know in the early days that Carrols Corporation, the largest franchiser in all of Burger King, would control almost all Burger King stores within 30 miles of Buffalo? The same was true, perhaps to a lesser extent, for both Arby's and Wendy's. As I researched and began to understand the broad web of control, I became increasingly selective in my employment choices. Why? In the early days I was concerned about how much information was shared across stores. I had every reason to believe, for example, that all stores under the same franchise owner would have a common computer system. I had what turned out to be unrealistic fears that I might be discovered as having been employed in multiple stores over time, which would have led to the discovery of my research and literary intent (you see, writing a book about this project and my experiences had been my intention early on).

As it turned out, my concern was misplaced. I witnessed countless examples of what can be classified only as a gypsy culture within a subclass of fast food workers. They drifted from store to store getting easy employment until some form of behavior, or personal wanderlust, led to movement along to the next store. In my one Wendy's experience, I worked alongside one such migrant who proudly proclaimed it was her third Wendy's in the past year.

I needn't have worried about being discovered. Franchise operations seem to behave like independent fiefdoms—at least in personnel decisions. Nor does there appear to be a central registry of fast food workers maintained by corporate headquarters. There is no software program used by the franchises or the corporations designed to pick up suspicious patterns of employment. All my paranoia was for naught.

Even though I didn't want to work in stores from the same franchiser, I did want to work at in at least two stores from the same corporation but run by different franchisers—my final rule. This would allow me to get a feel for the extent of influence wielded by corporate headquarters over their franchises. Of the seven restaurants, I worked at two Burger Kings and two McDonald's. I wanted to know if the big boys are actually able to command thousands of stores,

FROM BEHIND THE COUNTER

Elaine is notorious for starting food fights with favored coworkers. A bit of this had been tolerated because Elaine is a hard worker and she's reliable. But when the food fights escalated to knife tosses, management stepped in. Twice in the past this had happened to Elaine. She was rumored to be at this Wendy's only because of her friendship with the store manager.

spread across the world, to operate in relatively the same way. And if so, how do they do it?

My short answer to this tough question? Corporate headquarters exerted considerable control over operating procedures but not as much control over personnel procedures. Within one chain, across different states and timezones, a BK Whopper was cooked the same way. A McDonald's Quarter Pounder had the same garnishes applied the same way. I'm told there are procedural manuals governing operations that are hundreds of pages thick. There were big variations, though, in how people were hired, trained, and motivated.

Having established where I would seek employment, I created a set of simple rules for myself so that I could maintain my clandestine activities without raising suspicion:

1. Be truthful and be myself—to a degree.

2. Don't talk back.

3. Fit in; don't draw attention to myself.

So these were my basic rules—ones I tried to live by.

* * *

For the most part, my application and subsequent

employment were aboveboard. The only lie I told was that of omission. I didn't want people's behavior to change because I was doing research for a book, so I simply didn't tell them. Everything else was, well, the real me. I did have some trouble in the early application stages because I listed my job as "university professor." When no one showed any interest, I changed the wording of my occupation to "college teacher." Maybe in the minds of store managers, this was just one step up from a high school teacher—a group that at least one of my managers had had considerable experience hiring. Each application also asked for the salary on my last job. At first I was forthright in including this. As a public employee in New York State, my salary is a matter of record, identifiable by any student with the curiosity to find the published list in the school library. Naively, I entered my actual salary. Only after striking out with my first five applications did I think to question my directness. Store managers make about $45,000. Their assistants earn about $10,000 less. When I compared my salary at the university to the managers' salaries, I wisely decided to just leave this question blank. Shortly thereafter my application began to spark some interest. And thus began my journey.

✳   ✳   ✳

By taking these jobs, I was one step closer to uncovering what went on behind the counter in fast food restaurants. And what I saw only increased my interest. In slow times, fast food stores can look quite congenial, with crew members standing in groups of two or three, talking, sometimes laughing and for the entire world to see, enjoying themselves. During busy times, though, you see the drawn faces of people under pressure, yelling to or sometimes at each other, running from one place to another, trying to do more in less time.

To ensure that I gleaned as much detail as possible from each one of my jobs, it was important that I fit in. I needed to be like the other crew members and not draw attention to myself. People who know me thought this would be a high hurdle. Lots of professors like to be the center of attention. Imagine dozens of students congregated in a lecture hall architecturally designed to center on the person talking at the front of the room—you! People taking notes on every significant comment you make and being tested and graded on what you, and you alone, consider to be important concepts and facts. I've had 30 years of that kind of attention. Yes, it feels good to an admitted narcissist. As a side job, I also work as a consultant. People actually pay me money to hear what I have to say. It's a downright heady environment,

FROM BEHIND THE COUNTER

At 3 p.m., Phyllis, the night shift manager, arrives. She jokes with the crew, so she is well liked, but she can erupt into a tirade when confronted with something she finds particularly vexing. Enter Randy, who is standing around with seemingly nothing to do (which irks every manager, as best I can tell). Phyllis unleashes a flurry of abuse aimed at no one in particular (a popular way to give feedback) about the day crew never doing any of the countless chores that help transitions between shifts. She points to the grease filter over the deep fryers and insists that Randy begin cleaning them. When he gives her static about how "it's a day job," she becomes even more incensed: "When you're just standing around, you should be looking for things to do!" I'm taken aback at this outburst; the others seem to take it in stride.

and it's terrible preparation for being among the rank and file. In my fast food experiences, no one wanted to hear my opinion. My colleagues in the university were convinced this would be my undoing. Could I keep my mouth shut? I was committed to doing just that. I wanted to blend in, and as I quickly discovered, this meant not voicing my opinion on how work should be done.

For the most part I was successful. Twice I failed, and

one of those two failures probably almost got me fired. Fitting in meant I couldn't voice opinions about human resources practices. I couldn't, for example, point out that it was probably not good recruitment strategy to tell me, "You don't want this job. Go work somewhere else." I was given this advice by one shift supervisor who honestly thought he was saving me from a horrific experience. I also couldn't correct practices that were a violation or misinterpretation of existing laws.

Applying for a job at a Wendy's in Florida, this vow of silence cost me several hours of misery at a Social Security office. How? you ask. I came equipped to each job with a passport as proof of citizenship. Identification and proof of the right to work are employment hurdles that can be satisfied by a passport or by showing a driver's license and Social Security card. Wendy's wanted the latter and refused to accept a passport. Vowing to behave like any prospective crew member who might have also lost his or her Social Security card, I found myself locating the nearest Social Security office and waiting in line for a replacement card. The nearest office was 30 miles away in Jacksonville. The line, while not more than 20 people long, moved at a pace no self-respecting Wendy's employee would ever tolerate.

Fitting in didn't mean I had to strip myself of all vestiges of my personality, though. I resolved that I would behave normally but avoid indicating that I had any special knowledge. I am by nature gregarious and good humored. I make friends easily, and I vowed to continue this pattern wherever I worked and to make friends among my fellow crew members. To my

FROM BEHIND THE COUNTER

It's my second day at a Burger King, and I'm spending most of my time feeding hamburger and chicken into the famous BK grill, a large rectangular box that houses a wire mesh screen making a continuous loop between two flames. Food is placed on the grill and is flame broiled on both sides simultaneously. Quite ingenious, I thought when first I peered inside the inferno. Four hours later I am far less enthralled. The work, while not hard, is very hot, especially when you're tall and your face is exactly at the height of the flaming dragon's mouth. On the edge of heat exhaustion and convinced that I'm becoming dehydrated, I ask our store manager, Kris, for permission to take a break. Her reply is a curt "NO," unattended by any explanation. Somewhere in the second it takes for her to utter this answer, I misplace my steely resolve to behave just like any other crew member. Without thinking, I declare, "I know I'm supposed to clock out on the computer, so there really

surprise, though, at every place I worked I faced a huge invisible barrier to making friends. At first I thought it was an age difference. I was 57 at the time. Most of the people I worked with were one-third my age and younger than both my children. Surprisingly, the barrier even existed with the one or two older workers I found in most job sites. I'm con-

won't be any cost to you." Again she says "NO," this time with more emphasis but with no more explanation.

This just plain makes me mad. There wouldn't be any cost, and we are at a slow period, having completed the lunch rush some 45 minutes earlier. I persist, pointing out a fact she had offered during my interview: "You're on a profit-sharing plan. That means any labor costs you can avoid go straight into profit. So it's to your advantage to let me take a break." Big mistake. In her defense, she doesn't respond by firing me. Instead, she says that if I am tired, I should clock out and go home. And I do just that, angry that I have had to ask permission to take a short break and angry that this request was denied. Of course, by the time I get home I am kicking myself for having violated my own rule. Even worse, leaving early, no matter how sincere Kris's offer might have been, left the store possibly short-handed. Returning the next morning, I believe my chances of being fired are 50/50, but Kris doesn't say anything about yesterday. This close encounter only reinforced my resolve to fit in.

vinced now, after encountering the same barriers everywhere and seeing them dissolve in a similar fashion, that the problem wasn't age but rather turnover. The typical store I worked in had about 40 workers at any one time, half of whom had been there a year or more. The rest were transients, many quitting so quickly that they didn't bother, or were perhaps too embarrassed, to pick up their paychecks. Why bother to learn the name of someone or become friendly with someone who was about to leave? You seldom make friends of those people you meet in a revolving door, I reasoned.

In each of my jobs I found that congeniality increased the longer I stayed. During the first two or three days I seldom got more than a grunt in response to my chipper greetings. When I didn't bail on the first day and seemed to show no outward signs of leaving on the second, the thaw began. By the end of my second week, at least at the store with the lowest turnover (and, lending support to my thesis, also the one with the fewest strangers), I found people talking to me about what they did at night, what kinds of plans they had for getting out of fast foods, and other subjects much closer to my earlier expectations.

It did seem reasonable for me to voice opinions about things for which I had no special knowledge—operations kinds of issues. This was consistent with my personality. I am naturally curious and always interested in why things are done in certain ways and, as a result, why they aren't done differently. Plus, this was a *research* project, and it required a certain level of investigation. Why, I asked one day at my first BK job, wasn't there a bin to catch buns when they came shooting out of the continuously circulating toaster? You fed buns in the top, they were exposed to the heating element, and then they came shooting out the bottom and plunged toward the floor. There is no seven-second rule in fast food. If it falls, it's garbage. I'd guess I lost maybe 5 to 10 rolls a day. By my second day, I began to ask why there wasn't a better design, maybe a recessed bin in which buns could accumulate. Questions—and suggestions like these—most often fell on deaf ears. The typical response was: "This is the way we've always done it." In my experience, operations manuals were cast in concrete. No one challenged them. Even though I quickly learned that operating procedures were immutable, I was frustrated by a culture that wouldn't allow the established way to be challenged.

The one constraint on my friendliness was, of course, discussing why I was there in the first place—my research project. In my first two jobs crew members were curious about why I was working fast foods. Both of these jobs were local Buffalo operations, and it must have seemed strange to have a university professor from a school everyone knew working at their store. When asked, I found that most times it was sufficient to say I just loved that type of work, and it kept me busy in my early stages of retirement. One particularly perceptive kid, though, challenged my standard response, "No, really, why are you here?" After I again gave him the standard response, he returned the next day with a diagnosis unveiling my worst fears, "You're writing a book, aren't you?" Despite my disclaimers, he persisted with this all too correct observation. Fortunately, in later jobs my past credentials seemed to be far less a topic of discussion.

Two parts of my activities weighed heavily on me

mentally. The first was starting the job. There is a certain sameness to starting every job that I suspect you don't notice unless you begin lots of jobs in a short time frame. I had to watch DVDs that were boringly similar. How many times can you watch 20 minutes on proper hand-washing procedures before you're ready to scream? The other difficult part of the job was quitting. I'm not by nature a quitter. After all, I've been in the same job for 30 years and married for 37. By the very nature of this research project, though, I had to quit one job to start another. I tried in the beginning to work a second job while I was still employed at a first. While I probably could have handled the physical part of it, trying to schedule hours for multiple jobs was harrowing.

Not only was it against my nature to quit, but I also felt an obligation to the stores that had hired me in good faith. Several stores asked me to sign what I came to call an "At Will" document, which informed me that I was working in an At Will state and that I could be fired for any reason or no reason. I could also quit for any reason or for no reason. I guess this should have made me more comfortable with quitting, but I never was; so before starting this project, I decided to quit each assignment at a time that would minimize disruption. I gave as much notice as possible before quitting. I violated this rule twice: in my first job at Arby's and again at my last assignment when back problems became an issue. In the case of Arby's, there just wasn't enough business to warrant being fully staffed. I was hired in the dead of a Buffalo winter, and by my second week the daily high temperatures were in the 10°F to 15°F range. This, coupled with the usual Buffalo snow, left most people think-

THE RULES OF THE GAME

ing twice about venturing out. My store manager, Don, kept calling me, usually just an hour before my scheduled starting time, to tell me not to report: "Not enough business today, Jerry, sorry." After the third straight day of this, even Don seemed a bit contrite: "Sorry, Jerry, I'm going to have to cancel you again, but I promise it won't happen Thursday" (my next scheduled day). I decided at that time, after talking with some of my colleagues, that no employee dependent on a weekly paycheck would tolerate a job with such uncertain hours. If Don called and canceled again, I decided, I was going to quit. Sure enough, that's exactly what happened.

The only other time I quit without a minimum of two days' advance was due to back trouble. My back had been bothering me in each of my last three jobs, but I had just attributed it to a heavier physical routine coupled with almost constant bending over at workstations designed for people much shorter than I am. My third day at Krystal, I spent the entire shift bent over a grill, head and back in unnatural positions to avoid hitting an overhead sprinkler system installed at a height of six feet two inches. I left work in pain, which only worsened over the next two days. On the third day, my first scheduled since the back problems had escalated, I finally had to admit I wasn't going to be able to walk, let alone complete a normal shift. I called and quit four hours before my shift started. While my store manager was very understanding and my reasons medically sound—weeks later I would be diagnosed with three herniated discs and spend almost nine months rehabbing my way back to some normalcy—I still felt that I was letting the crew down.

I also decided I needed a neutral reason for quitting. I didn't want to give a reason that suggested something was wrong with the operations of the store I worked in or betray any dissatisfaction that might even remotely reflect badly on the management team. Fortunately, or I should say unfortunately, a series of serious illnesses befell close members of my family during that period. These personal crises gave both neutral and adequate reason for leaving the remaining five jobs.

* * *

I tried one other little experiment in this 14-month odyssey. While I was telling my Human Resources Management class about my fast food experiences, one of my students volunteered that he had worked at a Burger King for over two years. I briefly enlisted him to work at the same Burger King I will shortly identify as the best run of all my stores. The only catch—I wanted him to work on a different shift than I had worked. Why? you ask. If my day shift was extremely well managed, I ventured, shouldn't some of the same practices carry over to the night shift? And shouldn't, then, that shift also show above-average efficiency? It probably should have, but it didn't: Greg worked several weeks on the night shift of this Burger King. Having worked at another Burger King in this same franchise chain, Greg pronounced this shift far less effective. To illustrate his point, he described the favorite downtime activity—seeing who could put their head under the shake machine and last the longest before an icy headache forced surrender. While operating practices were consistent across stores and across shifts, personnel practices apparently didn't carry over, even between shifts. Explaining why became part of my quest.

The McJob Isn't McEasy

Supersized Management Principle

Self-worth is rarer and more fragile than we think. Good managers are ego architects. Building self-worth translates directly into commitment and productivity.

All managers face financial constraints. There is no inexhaustible source of money to motivate workers, and nowhere is this reality more evident than in fast food restaurants. Instead, the good managers rely on a currency they have control over: recognition for work well done and for jobs mastered. Although this is an old bromide extolled in every management text, the actual method fast food managers use for recognition is different from anything I've seen, and it is clearly effective in building employee self-worth. Good fast food managers recognize top performers by presenting them as models to emulate. If an employee demonstrated being the best at floor mopping or potato frying, when it came time for new employees to learn these tasks, he or she was glorified as the standard of excellence. No generalized trainer gave training tips across the range of tasks. Rather, different individuals were anointed as the bearer of standards for different tasks, responsible for conveying correct procedure and, as a reward, basking in the recognition that came with the special status. Far more than ordinary recognition programs, this excellence modeling concept significantly affected self-worth.

* * *

One of the goals in fast food is to make jobs behind the counter as easy as possible, which in part helps justify the low salaries. There is a limit to easy, though, and I'll try to demonstrate that here. The worst store managers I worked for, and indeed the crew members who followed their lead, subscribed fully to the "easy-job" description. I was told countless times, "This job is simple" or "You'll pick this up in no time" or, my favorite, "If you can't learn this job, we'll ship you to the home." This credo was terribly dysfunctional. Being told a job was simplicity itself and then finding that it was actually difficult to learn regularly sent me off with wounded self-esteem. Fortunately, I had done enough in my life—and had enough triumphs—that I knew if I was struggling, there was probably a reason for it outside of its being *me*. I certainly didn't have that level of self-awareness back when I was 18. It's important to realize that about half of the people I worked with during this time were in the age range of 18 to 25, and many of them lacked the self-awareness to know it wasn't necessarily their fault when things didn't go easily. Why is there such high turnover in the first few weeks of fast food jobs? Because we're told the job is easy, and then we struggle to meet even minimum standards. Those of us who haven't built ego shields leave much the worse for psychological wear. It is demoralizing to fail at a job everyone insists is easy.

Let's take some of these easy jobs and see how a good leader instilled self-worth. The task was sweeping and mopping. I admit this isn't a terribly complex task. But self-worth isn't a function of difficulty. Rather, it accumulates because someone convincingly demonstrates they value what you've done or how you've done a task. The first time I had to do

FROM BEHIND THE COUNTER

It's my third day at Krystal, and James, the store manager, wants me to learn how to assemble and wrap the different breakfast menu items. He points to an item on the point-of-sale (POS) screen that looks to me like "s. gr. scram." He then whips out a cup and starts putting ingredients in—following a prescribed order that I know I should try to pick up. Eureka! It's got sausage, and gravy, and eggs. I'll bet those words on the POS screen mean "sausage gravy scrambler." Before I can pat myself on the back, James is on to the next item. For the next 10 minutes a whirlwind of activity produces half a dozen different items, some assembled multiple times, others only once. James then says, "Jerry, why don't you try the next one?" I can read the disappointment on his face when I grab for the wrong cup, open the wrong warmer bin, and generally mess up the order. If you give me 10 minutes to learn 6 different things by watching rather than doing, I guarantee I will fail. In retrospect, I attribute the failure to poor training, but I suspect more than a few newbies wonder what is wrong with them. Yet even for those new employees who learned quickly, there is little ego gratification. After all, they *should* have done well. The job is McEasy, isn't it?

this seemingly easy task, Kris said to me in a voice louder than normal (probably, in retrospect, to make sure all crew members could hear), "Watch Ming Hoh. He is very good at this job, and he will show you how to do it." I thought to myself, "You put the mop in water, you drain off the excess water, you swab the deck. I've watched Navy war movies. I can do this. Why is she telling me to watch Ming Hoh?"

Ming Hoh was all over me for the next two days. Every time I swept and mopped, he followed up with advice: "You need to bend more and get under low tables. You've missed a sandwich wrapper." Never mind that the wrapper was wedged under a heavy metal drum. Never mind that it looked like it had been there since pterodactyls soared above the earth. Never mind that dozens of people probably missed the same wrapper before me. For Ming Hoh, all the people who had gone before me were irrelevant. I had not done my job right, and Ming Hoh told me, in a combination of Cambodian and English, that this was not acceptable. Kris had built self-worth by making Ming Hoh the keeper of the behavior standards. There were right behaviors and wrong behaviors, and she gave Ming Hoh tangible evidence that she valued his work. Looking back with a jaundiced eye, I might be tempted to conclude that Kris was being devious and manipulative, or perhaps that Ming Hoh was just easily manipulated. I don't think this was the case, though. Kris regularly "anointed" others as keepers of standards, and the response was always genuine and positive. For example, it was time for me to learn sandwich assembly, and Kris proudly noted that Daniel could assemble and wrap a sandwich in under 25 seconds. This started an alpha male ritual with others trying to top Daniel's time. The contest ended in a fictional crowning of Daniel as top in the shift. Kris walked away with a smile on her face. She knew we would be watching Daniel closely for behavioral clues: What was he doing that made him so fast? Kris had both praised Daniel's accomplishments and set a goal in sandwich assembly to which others could aspire.

I'm proud to admit I even succumbed to Kris's talents. Over the course of three days spent toasting rolls, I took satisfaction in making two or three timesaving adjustments that, while counter to the "Holy Operations Manual," were readily accepted as part of the norm. When Kris appointed me to teach a newbie how to toast, I behaved very much like Ming Hoh. The new Angus Burger's oversized roll had to be flattened between my two palms to fit successfully in the toaster. Be certain that I watched closely to make sure the newbie followed my directions. However minor my role, I was helping to pass along the cultural norms.

In Kris's eyes, every worker in her charge had a role, and correct behavior that led to good performance was to be acknowledged. If you wanted to work for her, you had to survive a lengthy interview and much behavioral scrutiny during training that sent a powerful signal—this job isn't McEasy, and only the best can work for me.

Now contrast this with the standard managerial practice. Training isn't assigned to an anointed role model, but rather to a generalized trainer, frequently a manager or assistant. Picture this on the first day of work because it's exactly what

I faced my first day working at a McDonald's in Michigan. I was scheduled to start at 10 a.m. I reported to the store manager, and we spent the first 12 minutes entering my name, address, Social Security number, and so on, into the computer. Then, without so much as a minute of training, I was put on the front counter! Allen, an assistant manager with nine months' tenure, was assigned to teach me. My job was to welcome customers, take their orders and enter those orders into the point-of-sale register-computer, announce the cost, and make change when handed payment by the customer. Allen's idea of training was the same as I had experienced in most of my first four fast food jobs—hands-off. Yes, this was my fifth job, and by then I should have been, if not a seasoned veteran, at least competent. Even though the people who hired me thought this was the first time I'd worked fast food, I should have known from my past experiences that I could do this job. After all, it's easy, right?

Merriam-Webster recently included *McJob* as an entry in its dictionary. The definition isn't flattering—words like "low-paying" and "dead-end" punctuate the description. The McDonald's response to this newest word in our vocabulary is, though, telling for its vehemence. In an open letter to Merriam-Webster, McDonald's labeled the definition as "an inaccurate description of restaurant employment" and "a slap in the face to the 12 million men and women" who work in restaurants.[1] They even went so far as to note that "more than 1,000" franchise owners "got their start by serving

---

[1] www.cnn.com/2003/SHOWBIZ/books/11/08/mcjob.dictionary.ap/, retrieved August 2, 2006.

customers behind the counter." To me all this sounded like an overreaction brought on by a fear that maybe the dictionary got it right. Indeed, the employees I worked with often dismissed their jobs, saying, "You'll get it in no time. Anyone could do it." Well, maybe I'm slow-witted. Maybe I'm weaker, frailer, and older than I think. I am here to say that the McJob is many things, but it isn't McEasy. I know easy. I've spent a lifetime seeking and surviving in easy. Jobs can be physically easy, and they can be mentally easy—and I've done both. In my 30 years as a university professor, my hardest physical task was having to carry a stack of 60 exams to class, a distance of over 300 yards.

I've also mastered mentally easy jobs, thank you very much. As a kid, I helped put myself through college by working on an assembly line in Wixom, Michigan. I built Lincolns. Or, more accurately, I pressed a button on a spot welder 11 times to join two pieces of metal together. Once every 55 seconds or so, I spent 15 seconds pushing a button—all day, every day. The job took me 10 minutes to learn and 10 hours to master. I admit I can be slow at times; some employees learned jobs similar to mine more quickly. But after I learned the task, I learned how to daydream, and that was the only thing that helped me survive a truly "easy" job.

It's tempting to say that fast food jobs are easy both physically and mentally, but please resist that urge. Every fast food job I worked was harder physically than being a professor. Many of them were also harder than my assembly-line work, and this was an assembly job that seasoned veterans avoided if possible. They used to give spot welding to the new kids on the line. If you go into a car plant today, you will see robots doing those jobs. People don't want to do them, and I suspect neither do the robots, but they complain a lot less.

Fast food is certainly more mentally demanding than working on an assembly line. On the line, I simply had to learn how to press a button and where to put my 11 welds. Very few fast food jobs were this mentally unchallenging. For example, working the fryer—a typical first job—involved nine steps:

1. Open a bag of fries.

2. Fill the basket about half full. (At McDonald's, a machine did this step because we humans might have made a mistake. But at most places, this task was done manually.)

3. Place the basket in the deep fryer.

4. Push the timer button to track the cooking time.

5. Play Pavlov's dog: Remove the basket from the fryer when the buzzer rings (ding, fries are done!) and tip it so the fries go into the holding tray. Be careful: It takes two hands to tip it accurately so that hot grease doesn't start flying about. Don't spill even a drop of grease on the floor, or you will be skating—not walking—in it for the rest of the day.

6. Salt the fries.

7. Push another button that signals when seven minutes were up, which was the "suggested hold time" for fries.

8. Check the screen for the size of fries requested on the next order.

9. Fill the corresponding fry container with fries and place it in the holding bin.

It *sounds* easy. And I grant you, cooking french fries was probably easier to learn and to do than making 11 spot welds. But when you account for the environment in which these jobs were learned and performed, maybe this easiest-of-fast-food jobs wasn't quite so painless. The temperature under the fry warming light was about 160°F, not exactly air-conditioned luxury. During the lunch rush you filled one fry container not every 55 seconds—as was the case with my spot welds on cars—but about once every 5 seconds. When not filling fry containers, you were trying to keep several fry baskets going in the deep fryer at the same time. Oh, did I mention that fries weren't the only thing fried in fast food restaurants? Of course you knew that! Chicken nuggets, anyone? Jalapeño peppers? Onion rings? Every fast food restaurant had several items requiring a deep fryer. After all, trans fats taste good. The fry guy's job was to keep all these things in ready supply. Remember those guys who'd spin plates on top of long poles on *The Ed Sullivan Show*? Like that.

Still, you argue, this isn't brain surgery. What's so hard about a fast food job? Remember, "fry guy" is the job they

FROM BEHIND THE COUNTER

A customer orders a medium Diet Coke. I have to find the medium-drink button, touch it, then find the Diet Coke button and touch that. If he wants no ice, well, I don't know what to do with "no ice." If I personally fill the order, I give no ice or I ask the runner to give no ice. And if it is a senior citizen who wants this drink and requests the senior discount, either I touch the generic-discount button after touching the medium-drink and type-of-drink buttons, or I locate the special-senior-discount button.

Whatever the button, I am hopelessly lost in minutes. "Have it your way" makes me want to go far, far away. Sure, I can do the simple things, like handling the seasoned customer who asks for a senior coffee and, upon seeing my distress, reaches over the counter and from an upside down position points out the button for me to hit. *That* was easy!

usually teach you first. It's the easy one. But, you say, it's not brain surgery. That's true. And neither is counter work in and of itself. Maybe the difficulties in how these jobs are learned and mastered will become a bit clearer if we go back to my first day with Allen.

Keep in mind that fast food places don't have old-fashioned cash registers anymore. They have point-of-sale register-computers that have all the names of items on the face of a computer screen. Touch the screen with your finger and the corresponding item appears in the "order box," which is an isolated area off to the side of the screen designed to keep a running tally of a customer's order and its cost. Now if this sounds easy, it isn't. Even with Allen watching from behind me, I needed almost constant attention to find the right buttons.

Now let's add another source of pressure. Remember, this was still my first day, and I was about one hour into my "training." Training wasn't too scary, despite the hieroglyphics on the touch screen, as long as I had only an occasional customer and trustworthy Allen was right behind me to correct any mistakes. But by 11:15 there wasn't just the occasional customer—there was a steady flow such that Allen was no longer standing directly behind me. He was at his own register! Having decided I could fly solo, he deserted me with words to the effect that he would answer any questions I had. As the lines got longer, though, Allen had his own pressures. And answering my increasingly frequent questions only added pressure to his job. While he tried to help, his body language was screaming "LEARN IT YOURSELF!"

It's amazing how normally nice people become impatient when they pick a line, hoping it will be faster than the alternative choices—only to discover they are guinea pigs for the latest trainee. After all, this is supposed to be *fast* food. That first day I was anything but fast. The volume level of muttering in my line was getting louder, and it didn't take too long before Allen called one of the experienced workers up. I felt as though I had failed. No one told me that this was an expected part of the training program—I found this out for myself when the next trainee performed even worse. And neither of us had a designated role model. Allen wasn't nominated for this job. It wasn't a source of pride for him to see me succeed. There were no Ming Hohs or Daniels, part of whose self-worth was linked to my success. Rather, there was Allen, whose primary job was to get product out the door, and if I experienced some failure, it was a normal part of the job. For $6.50 an hour, they throw in a humiliating experience at no extra charge. I left that day exhausted and depressed. How could I have wilted under what others characterize as an "easy" job? "Maybe the job isn't so McEasy," I thought.

Over the 14 months of this project, I was exposed to seven nonsupervisory jobs that appeared in one form or another in each of my restaurants, and I was expected to learn them all. Fast food restaurants place a premium on flexibility. Workers who won't—or can't—learn all the tasks are treated as second-class citizens. At a Burger King in Buffalo, New York, I met one woman named Marsha who resisted learning any but the easiest jobs in the store. She cleaned tables in the front and washed dishes in the back. Anything else seemed to scare her—the pace was too quick, the steps too complex. The store manager, ever the efficiency expert, clamored for Marsha to learn other things. When she wouldn't, her hours were gradually reduced. In my last days at that location, Marsha was averaging less than five hours per week. One day after my shift, I sat down in the store and talked to her while she was waiting for a ride home. She didn't understand why she wasn't getting more hours, and she feared that the new mobile home she shared with her mother and husband was beyond her financially. Months later I saw her at a local Wal-Mart. She was the front-end greeter. I guess she got the message.

What were my seven jobs, you ask? I'll tell you.

1. The Front Counter. This is the job I just described. It was actually easier than the same job performed at the drive-thru window. Drive-thru was harder for two reasons: First, the headphones and speaker systems were straight out of *The Flintstones*. The crackles of static, the silence of missed words, and the variety of accents that people bring to the order window made interpretation of orders a most difficult task. There was also the occasional really "trying" customer, such as the one reported recently on myjobsucks.com, wherein an experienced window crew member recounts the story of a customer whose order she could not hear, despite several interruptions requesting the customer to speak louder. Perhaps it was the rain falling in buckets outside, she reasoned, that caused only a faint mumble to be heard through the headphones. Finally she traced the problem. It seemed the customer had closed the window to avoid the rain and was placing the order from inside the sealed car. Also, drive-thru was hard because fast food restaurants pay particular attention to *drive time*. This is the time it takes from order completion to customer receipt. By a considerable margin

---

FROM BEHIND THE COUNTER

A Burger King I worked at in Florida was having trouble with its drive times. I knew this because the franchise owner installed an electronic message board that kept flashing two directives: "If You Have Time To Lean, You Have Time To Clean." And the much less subtle: "People, We Need To Reduce Our Drive Times."

(some store managers reported a 70 to 30 spread), more business is done at the drive-thru window than inside the store. Everyone from the district manager through the vice president of franchise operations pays attention to drive times, and store managers who don't meet acceptable standards face considerable pressure from above.

2. THE SANDWICH BOARD. Every sandwich had to be assembled, and the way in which this was done was strictly monitored. Wendy's burgers had a W autographed in mustard as the last step before a bun covered up and smudged the masterpiece. Whopper Juniors got two pickles. Regular Whoppers got three. Fish filets at McDonald's got one-half slice of cheese. Learning all the different rules of order, most designed to maximize speed, took time. And under pressure of getting out a burger, especially with the special orders that supposedly didn't upset us, the job could wear you down. As evidence, the most likely place for tempers to flare was on the sandwich boards. Literally everyone else either supplied this job or waited for the end product from this effort. This was what we sold: The burger stops here.

When the rush was at its peak, the very best assemblers became king (or queen) of the hill. They took over from slower assemblers who controlled the board during off-peak hours. They even had an unwritten right to argue with a manager when their speed or accuracy was called into question; otherwise, as I've noted earlier, insubordination of this type was rarely tolerated. I recall one aggressive exchange that took place between Orville, the assistant manager at a Wendy's in Florida, and Elaine, the top assembler. Orville often worked as a runner during lunch rush. When Orville had an order that wasn't yet completed, he would often step in and ask the assembler to bump him to the front of the queue. One especially busy Friday, Elaine had had enough: "Orville, you always do this! I've got a screen full of orders to fill, and I'm doing them in the order they come in, so stop trying to get special treatment." Orville sputtered back, but he chose not to take her on. Maybe it was because Elaine was right, or maybe it was because the assembler job was key, and Elaine was the best.

3. THE FRY GUY. This was typically the first job newbies were assigned, and the task varied in difficulty from chain to chain. McDonald's sells a ton of fries—so many more than other chains that they actually have a semiautomated assembly line for dispensing fries into baskets. A crew member

poured multiple bags of frozen fries into a large hopper. An empty basket came up the line and hit a trigger plate, and a predetermined amount of fries dropped into the basket, ready for a later date with the deep fryer. Wendy's also had a fry station, and the combination of fries, chicken nuggets, and fried chicken sandwiches, all with different cooking times, made the first couple of days on this job both tiring and hot. Burger King doesn't seem to sell as many fries, or at least so it seemed to me. But they did sell chicken and onion rings that were deep fried. Despite this, they didn't assign someone full-time to the fry station. Rather, on an as-needed basis, as dictated by near-empty bins, someone with a moment to spare assumed this responsibility. The same was true at Arby's. Even though they had fried chicken sandwiches, fried onion petals, fried Jalapeño peppers, *and* fried mozzarella sticks, the job apparently didn't warrant a full-time worker, except in the busiest of times.

4. THE RUNNER. Some stores had register people who both rang up the orders and then filled them. At least during busy times, though, most stores used runners. They would read the order on the screen, then look for the sandwich portion of the order as it was transferred to a holding bin by an assembler. Then they combined sandwich, fries, drinks, condiments, cutlery, and napkins into an order that went into a bag for drive-thru or onto a tray for eat-in service. The hardest parts of this job were remembering which orders had been completed, remembering which orders were only partially done and what was still needed to complete them, and ensuring quality control. On occasion, and it was less rare than it should have been, customers had left the drive-thru window and traveled miles down the road, only to discover the Double Whopper they had ordered was a fish filet sandwich. At a Wendy's I worked in, one of these errors led to a screaming session between a violently angry customer and a store manager. (Crew members were trained to bounce complaints up to the manager. Still, they typically were the object of the first angry barrage—remember this book's Introduction?) This customer was so incensed by the order mistake that he backtracked several miles on the expressway to unleash his anger. No one makes enough money in a fast food job to bear the amount of abuse that this customer leveled that day.

5. The Cook. What a crock! Neither McDonald's nor Burger King had a "cook." Technology has all but eliminated this job. Picture a giant Foreman grill. Standing about four feet off the ground and measuring maybe three feet by two feet, the grill had a series of buttons on the front corresponding to the different menu items that needed to be grilled. Need eight burgers? Place the frozen burgers on the grill, push button 1, the grill top goes down, and about 40 seconds later the grill top opens to the smell of newly cooked hamburgers. At Burger King the grill was the first job rookies were assigned. Inside a rectangular box standing about seven feet tall was a conveyor belt constructed of heavy-duty mesh wire. Above and below the conveyor were two flames. Burgers were placed on this mesh, and they moved along the belt at a preset speed, were cooked on both sides simultaneously by the two flames, and then spilled out the other end into holding trays. The cook spent all day feeding burgers, chicken, and veggie patties into an opening about 8 inches by 18 inches. When the conveyor was loaded, the "cook" toasted rolls and placed them in a warming bin.

At Wendy's they still had that quaint notion that people should cook the burgers.[2] Because of my several years of short-order-cooking experience, I was rotated into the cook position after only two days on the fry job. Even though I knew how to cook a burger, I didn't know how to cook it the "Wendy's way." Whether cooking a single or a junior burger, there was a way to put the burger on the fry surface (load from back to front) and to salt it (salt from front to back). There was a way to pat down the burger (touch each of four quadrants in succession—the order of which is a corporate secret). Wendy's insisted that every burger had to be in one of three states of readiness, and there had to be some burgers at each stage of completion:

> *Stage 1.* Raw patties just beginning to cook
>
> *Stage 2.* Burgers flipped once and soon to be ready
>
> *Stage 3.* Cooked burgers waiting for assembly into sandwiches

This job was fun because not only did I get to cook but I also got to anticipate how many orders were coming in at what

---

2 Much to my disappointment, Wendy's now also uses a Foreman-type grill to cook burgers.

time of day. Underestimate and customers got angry with the wait; overestimate and burgers were overcooked. Wendy's had a picture of a burger that was too well done to sell, and it was not a pretty picture. These burgers were retired to a warming tray, where they were used in the next day's batch of chili. In spare moments at Wendy's, the cook was also in charge of grilling chicken, baking potatoes, and emptying grease traps.

The last store I worked at was a southern chain called "Krystal," where every burger was cooked by human hands. Krystal is a kissing cousin to White Castle, so they deal in volume sales of tiny little burgers sold at very low prices. From the first day I was the cook at Krystal. This was less fun than the Wendy's cooking job because of the sheer volume. Krystal had four grills going at peak periods (a fifth was broken). On Fridays at rush hour these four grills were completely filled with burgers about an eighth of an inch thick and two inches square, smothered in onions and covered by buns to allow them to steam and be infused with the onion taste. As fast as I filled a grill with burgers, smothered them with onions, and covered each with a bun, I would move to the next grill and take completed burgers off for assembly and boxing. At my very best and at optimal speed, I was not quite as fast as the customers, many of whom ordered packs of 10 or 20 "to go." You might think a pack of 20 would serve a good-sized family reunion, but in reality customers regularly bragged that they ate 5 or more at a sitting.

6. SPECIALTY PREP. All the new salads and other variants of nontraditional items (for example, chili, oven-baked cookies, biscuits) had to be either assembled for refrigeration or prepared for cooking. This job didn't have the same level of pressure as the others, but it did require someone who was a self-starter. In my experience, this job went to older workers who had a measure of self-discipline but who wouldn't have tolerated the more hectic pace in the other jobs. I guess I should feel happy that at 57 years old, I never had to do this job on a regular basis.

7. MAINTENANCE AND STOCKING. Every facility I worked in had a jack-of-all-trades. When deliveries came with supplies, he (it was always a *he*) helped unload the truck and stocked goods in the freezers, coolers, or staples cabinets and/or on shelves. When machines broke down, this was the guy who was able to either fix the machine or determine that a specialist was needed. Frequently this job was manned by a more senior person. Usually it was afforded great deference: Even store managers didn't mess with the maintenance guy.

Besides these seven jobs, there were dozens of little tasks that had to be learned at fast food restaurants. And because they were fairly simple to learn and often undesirable to perform, they frequently fell to the newest person to learn and master as a spare-time "filler" task. I called them "fillers" because we were supposed to do them during slow times. I

FROM BEHIND THE COUNTER

While working in a McDonald's in Michigan, I witnessed a tiff between the maintenance guy and the sandwich assemblers. One day, the maintenance guy didn't feel as though he was getting the proper respect. Right in the middle of lunch rush he walked out without as much as a "so long!" If you detect a hint of anger here, it's because he left *me* with a malfunctioning fry loader. I didn't discover this until the height of the lunch rush—and me with no fries to cook. Having worked in seven restaurants, I knew that unreliability was the single least tolerated shortcoming in most of the jobs. Any other worker in any other job would have been fired immediately, but this fellow came back the next day and nothing was said, as best I could determine. Some jobs were clearly more vital than others.

guess there is nothing worse than idle hands at $6.50 an hour. So I learned how to sweep and mop floors the Burger King Way (different brooms and mops for behind and in front of the counter; start at 11 o'clock in the back and work all the way around the circle). I also learned how to wash dishes, trays, and cutlery—only McDonald's had a dishwasher. At all the other places I worked, there was some form of human interaction, usually in the form of old-fashioned scrubbing followed by rinsing in a disinfectant solution. I also had to restock ketchup and mustard, fill ice machines, load malt machines, and complete dozens of jobs that would not make anyone's top-10 list for fun.

By the end of a first day, and certainly by the end of a first week, you have been deluged with new information. You have been worked nonstop. You have lifted, mopped, and wrapped until you are exhausted. And you've made less than $50 on all but the best days.

I'm living testament that this job is hard.

The Great Cheese Wars and Other Culture Tales from Behind the Counter

O f all the foes I have battled as a professor and consultant, culture is the most formidable. If you want to change the way people behave, you must first get around the 800-pound gorilla—culture. Every time crew members act in any situation, they are governed by either the formal rules already established by the company or the network of informal rules that sprout to cover the scenarios not anticipated in the company's expressed formal standards. Managers and companies simply can't establish protocols for every contingency. Instead, when uncertain, employees learn what to do by observing others and by listening to storied exploits of those colleagues they admire.

So how do managers influence these informal networks? According to the *Wall Street Journal*, they don't.[1] Downsizing and delayering apparently have claimed another casualty: mentoring. Managers simply don't have time to spend their days offering advice and guidance to employees. There are just too many employees, and too much skepticism about

---

1 Carol Hymowitz, "Today's Bosses Find Mentoring Isn't Worth the Time and Risk," *Wall Street Journal*, March 13, 2006.

motives, to do this. Remember, fast food is about cost, and unless the bottom line impact of an activity is apparent to a manager, the task gets low priority. Successful managers see the bottom line impact of maintaining a strong culture, buttressed by what I've referred to as a *sensei*. James at Krystal chose not to hire an assistant manager: "It's my way of keeping costs down; my bonus depends on it." Similarly, Kris at Burger King, working a much larger operation, had only one assistant manager on a shift. Yet both of these managers spent considerable time with me the first day or two, trying, I'm sure, to convey some of the most important informal rules that defined their cultures. But typically I found that managers didn't have time for more than the initial imprinting of a relationship. After all, turnover in this industry means there's a new crew member just around the golden arches, anxiously awaiting indoctrination. How, then, does the "seasoned" two-day employee learn the really important things of the operation? Good managers cultivate a *sensei*—someone who has mastered key skills and internalized the formal rules, whose social presence makes it easier to transmit the informal rules to new crew members. Let me tell you the story of Daniel, the *sensei* of Burger King.

One of my favorite managers, Kris, whom you met in Chapter 2, told me to work with Daniel because he was a top assembler. So I watched Daniel closely. What was so special about him? Yes, he was fast. But he also could be a bit flaky. We got through the first wave of lunch rush, and Daniel switched into an altogether different gear. From Daytona

FROM BEHIND THE COUNTER

One busy Friday, two days after my Whopper training, Kris is working drive-thru because the regular has the day off. This is a hard job, in my estimation the hardest, but Kris performs well and also helps bag orders for the front counter in her spare time. The only time she raises her voice in two solid hours of long lines is to say, "This is FAST food, people, emphasis on *fast!*" We get it, and we respond. But when things slow down, Kris breaks into a smile. Walking to the office where two workers, one an assistant manager, the other a reputed "fast gun" from the next shift, are joking around, she immediately joins in. Their laughter lightens the mood throughout the entire work area. Kris's actions are very much like Daniel's. This consistency between leader and *sensei* informs the overall culture in that Burger King. It is clear to me, and others, that camaraderie and a strong work ethic coexist quite well here.

500 fast, he shifted down to a speed just fast enough to avoid hearing every manager's favorite mantra: "*If you've got time to lean, you've got time to clean.*" And indeed, that's what Daniel did. But as he cleaned, he also talked to John, the assembler across the counter. Daniel and John were gamers, and they talked avidly about the secrets of conquering level

13 of some new computer game. I was quickly lost by the conversation, but I noticed with interest the bond between them. When asked to share his secret, Daniel sheepishly admitted it took him until three the prior morning to master what he is about to tell John.

The second wave hit, and Daniel calmly switched back into high speed, showing me exactly what Kris wanted me to learn. When Daniel was in coast mode he seemed to be the social glue. If he was not talking about computer games, he was tossing a Hacky Sack at unsuspecting coworkers. To be a target was an honor: You were accepted! Where did Daniel learn how to mix work with fun? I'm guessing from Kris, who nurtured this informal leadership talent.

The Managers

I thought all my fast food stores would be pretty similar. They weren't. Some stores made employees wear name tags, going as far as sending people home if they repeatedly didn't wear their name tags, while other stores didn't seem to care. In some stores crews socialized after work, but in others they barely talked to each other, even during work. Even though every chain had strict rules about every facet of food production and customer interaction, how employees were treated was part of an individual store culture, and this varied from store to store. These differences could often be traced to the managers' values and practices and how consistently they were applied both by the managers and by their *sensei,* much more so than any edicts from headquarters. The best-run store I worked at was the Burger King in the story above; the worst-run store was also a Burger King. If corporate rules had a controlling impact, shouldn't stores have been much more similar? At one McDonald's the employees were extremely friendly; at another the tension between groups was palpable. The differences, I think, can be traced to the managers. There were rules for how to make a burger, and they were quite specific and straightforward. Rules for how and when to give praise, or how to give feedback, were less clear, though. In general leadership and management practices were less consistent across stores. To build consistency during a shift, managers depended on their ability to find someone who accepted and transmitted key cultural expectations. The following is a sampler of the types of managers I encountered. Only the last group, performance managers, was good at finding a *sensei* and developing consistent people practices. Later in this chapter, I'll share with you profiles of the crew members I worked with.

The Toxic Manager

Most new employees learn through feedback. When you're first learning a job, there's relatively little ego involvement in feedback; good managers seem to know this and in early days of employment are quick to point out better ways of doing a task. Some managers, though, use sarcasm or disrespectful comments to indicate when they are unhappy with

FROM BEHIND THE COUNTER

Don's sarcasm seems to permeate the culture. When I call in an order, I accidentally say "chicken filly" instead of "chicken filet." Alec, the regular sandwich assembler, hears this and mocks my mistake in a barely audible tone: "Chicken filly? Are we serving horse here? What does a chicken filly sound like?"

your work. One of the worst offenders I ran into was the store manager at Arby's, who admitted that the main reason he was hiring me was to change the store culture. He said he was tired of employees who were vulgar and disrespectful, but it didn't take long for me to realize that the role model for their behavior was actually the manager himself—Don. His attitude and style set the tone for everyone else in his store. Almost as bad, the key individual with the necessary attributes to be a *sensei* shared Don's disregard for the feelings of others. Don, in particular, didn't confine his wrath to "bad" employees. Bill, a diligent long-timer, messed up a coupon order. A customer had an entertainment book coupon for one Value Meal free with the purchase of another. There was a labyrinth of steps to complete some of the discounts correctly. When Bill made the error, it was right before the end of Don's shift, and Don tore into him, saying loudly

FROM BEHIND THE COUNTER

Toxic managers breed contempt among the crew members—for the job and for each other.

We are getting low on potatoes, and I ask Orville where they are after checking every fridge and storage area. They're under the grill behind a box and not easily visible, especially for someone tall and with arthritis. Rather than pointing out where they are, he says, "What's the matter with you, man, can't you read?" He says this with something of a grin, but it's not at all funny.

I ask Orville for a break after working nonstop on the grill from 11 a.m. until almost 2:30. I'm hungry, tired, and have to go to the bathroom. He asks if I'd had one, and then he makes me wait 10 minutes more until someone gets off a cigarette break. When I finally get a break, I'm determined to eat as quickly as possible. I don't want Orville to have any call for anger. I'm gone less than 10 minutes. Nevertheless, when I come back, Orville says, supposedly in jest, "What was that, like a half hour?" Without thinking, I say, "How would I know? If I could tell time, would I be working fast food?" As the words come out, I try to reel them back in, sure that my mouth finally has done me in, I'm going to be fired . . . from a fast food job! Wrong again: Orville thinks it's hilarious. What gives?

enough for everyone to hear, "Well, I'm leaving before Bill can make my life any more miserable." It didn't take long to infect others with this lack of respect for employees.

At a Wendy's in Florida I ran into an even more disrespectful manager. But unlike Don's style in the store described above, Orville's style didn't permeate the place. Perhaps that was because as an assistant manager he had neither the formal manager title nor the *sensei* characteristics to command the respect of others. Fortunately, countering his style was a good store manager who gave wonderful feedback. Orville was an aberration, but a thoroughly disliked aberration, and like the other sarcastic managers I worked for, you did the work you had to, but you never did more than that.

The Mechanical Manager

The most common type of manager I encountered was the Mechanical Manager, who was for the most part either an assistant manager or a shift manager, not a full store manager. You could spot the Mechanical Managers from across the room—they did their jobs, day after day, as if fast food was slow death. They didn't want to be there, and they were just going through the motions. They typically had gotten their jobs because they were reliable crew members and had put in enough time that some reward was needed to keep them working. A promotion has a certain finality, though—it makes you confront reality: Is this what I want out of life? Most say "No," and that's probably why I didn't see very many store managers who were mechanical. Before most store managers had reached that level (one store manager told me it was a 10-year journey), those who weren't interested in fast food as a lifetime career had moved on to other career pursuits. While looking for other opportunities, though, they did what was necessary to get by. Luis at McDonald's was the perfect example.

In my first McDonald's experience I made myself a grid showing all of the sandwiches and their ingredients. After a day of having instructions blasted at me, I needed a visual training aid to finally put things together. I shared this grid with Luis on my third day, expecting he might already have training materials like this (as was the case at Wendy's) or that he could use it to train other visual learners. As I handed Luis the Excel spreadsheet, I watched his face and saw no reaction. None. He told me he'd leave it for Kris, the store manager. Clearly he saw the value in it—he didn't toss it, after all—but a reinforcing response for my initiative required a level of involvement he didn't or couldn't muster.

Most of the highest-level managers didn't fit into the mechanical category, but there was one exception, Angela, who certainly did. On my first day at this particular Burger King, no one greeted or acknowledged me. I had no idea who the manager was, although I knew she was on duty. The guy from second shift who had hired me explained that I'd be working for her. Neither I nor anyone else had a name tag. I felt like I was passing through a turnstile and that my coworkers saw no point in learning why I was there or who I

FROM BEHIND THE COUNTER

Today I ask Dana if indeed Angela is the manager, because she says almost nothing to anyone. Actually, I don't know this, but I do know it's my second day and she has said nothing to me. I still don't know what she looks like from the front side. Dana says maybe I don't want to know who she is because she talks to most of us only when she's angry. Apparently she has a quick and nasty temper.

It's my third day, and still most of the people don't even acknowledge me. No one wears name tags. I think it's a mistake not to wear name tags: Customers don't know who is waiting on them, and new employees have a harder time meeting people—it exacerbates the us-versus-them problem. Angela still says nothing to me.

I'm counting now. . . . It's my fourth day, and I decide the silent treatment has to end. Maybe it's not a silent treatment. Maybe it's not intentional and aimed at me, but rather a normal way of doing business! I hope not.

was. I finally learned from Dana, a coworker, that the manager's name was Angela. She pointed to the front end, where I could see a female with her back turned, working as a runner. This was all I saw or heard of Angela, even though I must have walked right by her at the beginning of this, my first shift.

FROM BEHIND THE COUNTER

Be careful what you wish for when dealing with dysfunctional management. My first exchange of more than "hello" with Angela is not a pleasant one. Water is dripping from the roof onto the work area during a heavy downpour. I put a bucket under one spot where the drips are hitting. I move over a bit, making my job awkward. There's a second leak, but a bucket isn't practical because it's a major walkway, so I decide to put down a paper towel to keep the footing from getting even more slippery. Angela at first doesn't see my solution, but about 15 minutes later she looks directly at me and utters only three words: "Pick it up." I protest a bit, saying if someone slips, she has a worker's compensation claim. She says nothing except "Pick it up." I pick it up. A bit later Amy tells me in a hushed

So on my fourth day, I conducted an experiment that went like this:

I walk in and say, "Hi, Judy" to the senior citizen who works the front counter. She whispers to me, "Goodness, it's nice to finally have someone say hello." I extend my experiment because Angela is five feet down the counter working the runner job as usual. "Hi, Angela." She hasn't spoken a word to me in three days, but the direct approach works. "Good morning," she says without turning toward me. I walk to the back where Amy is washing dishes. "Hello, Amy." No

tone to be careful—anything else and I'm going to be sent home for the day. I'm shaken. I also feel wronged. Would I really be in trouble for something like this? And should I have been able to read that Angela was that mad?

Later that week I find out that my daughter is going to need surgery for extensive polyps in her nose that might be cancerous. We're all terrified since cancer runs in the family. I go into work deciding it will be my last day. During a slow time, I decide to tell Angela that I am quitting, explaining that I have to take care of my daughter who is about to have surgery. She shows absolutely no emotion at this. She shows no concern at my obvious emotional state. She stops listening after I say I am quitting. When I say goodbye, there's no response. On the way out I tell Tammy and Judy that I am quitting, and thankfully their reactions are more humane.

response. Thinking it is possible she doesn't hear me, I sing out in my off-key way, "Good morning, Amyyyy." She ignores me. Not to be denied, I comment, "Well, if enthusiastic and happy doesn't work, how about . . ." and in my best attempt at a sexy voice I say smoothly, "Hello, Amy. How are you?" She laughs, but still no hello. Has everyone adopted Angela's unfriendly manner? Is this further evidence that managers convey culture? She seems a combination of both the toxic and mechanical manager.

FROM BEHIND THE COUNTER

James is pulling a 24-hour shift. When I ask why, he explains it's not uncommon, and he does it to accommodate schedule requests from some of the workers. He is very attuned to what hours people want to work, perhaps because these people aren't paid all that well. I've noticed at my two lowest-paying jobs, my first McDonald's and here, that getting people's hours right is key. When he tells me I am working six hours each on Saturday and Sunday after a six-hour shift today, I tell him I prefer not to work Sunday. He adjusts the hours immediately, explaining that because I wanted about 20 hours per week, he was trying to get them all from Friday to Sunday, which are my first three days and the last of the store's week.

After lunch rush James comes around and tells everyone their accumulated hours for the week so far. I think this routine is designed to check his totals for accuracy against crew expectations. This appears to be a regular event, although I've never seen any other manager confer with employees about anything.

The Relationship Manager

The Relationship Manager was a relatively rare breed in my experience. James was the prototype. He led by building relationships and demonstrating that he cared about our destinies—hard to do when it seemed like every week someone was leaving and another person was coming on board. From the first day, James was very different from what I was used to. When I first met him for my job interview, he was 15 minutes late because he was out picking up an employee whose car had broken down. I never saw any other manager pick up or take home a crew member who had transportation problems. In fact, at one store I watched Mary, an older worker teetering on the edge of poverty, sit in a booth out front for two hours waiting for her husband to pick her up after his shift at a Sam's Club. As I came to learn, this kindness wasn't unusual for James. And in being kind, James created a culture that was much more friendly and supportive than that in many of the other fast food places I had experienced. Even the way James responded to my quitting was refreshing. With my back problems becoming increasingly worse, I called James to tell him that I was quitting and dreaded leaving him in the lurch. But he was amazingly kind, telling me to take care of myself and forcefully telling me to pick up my check. What a far cry from Angela's behavior, who barely acknowledged my daughter's illness and who said nothing to inquire about her when I went back to get my last checks.

The Performance Manager

It's easy to spot the Performance Manager. Here relationships are still important, but now they serve as a means to ensure performance. Through word or deed she very quickly

FROM BEHIND THE COUNTER

But people also matter to Kris because when they're happy, they're productive. I don't know why Daniel is suddenly timing himself to see how fast he can put together a Whopper. "Nineteen seconds!" he declares, elated at his time. I ask if it's good. He proudly acknowledges yes. When I prod further, he admits three people are faster than he is: Kris, the manager, Alex, one of the assistant managers, and Craig, who has been working shifts other than mine. Daniel is a college graduate. Is being the best assembler his career aspiration? I don't think so. But it's clear that Daniel, more than anyone else, takes to heart Kris's insistence on performance.

Daniel tells me with considerable pride that this is the top Burger King store in the nation. A similar claim is made at my McDonald's, and I'm beginning to wonder if this isn't an urban legend started by managers. Clearly the people here care about being fast. Daniel says that people do the right thing because secret shoppers come around and grade them, and it's a matter of honor to do well.

lets you know what is expected. I like this. No ambiguity, no doubt about what it takes to make the grade. The best at this was Kris, who, it seemed to me, watched for slackers much more closely than did the managers at other fast food places.

She told me during the interview that I would be watching DVDs my first day. She also mentioned that one of the new people had taken three to four bathroom breaks while watching the videos, which was an excessive number, she thought. She also commented that she might be losing some people because she thought they were slower than they should be. I got the message: She would be watching my work and looking to see if I was going to goof off. My experience in other places was that you got fired for only two things: not showing up and insubordinate behavior. Clearly she was adding a third reason—poor performance. Good for her!

Kris's watchful eye extended beyond bathroom breaks. I found out the hard way that taking breaks, even unpaid ones, wasn't allowed, unless legally required. Apparently in New York State, you're not entitled to a break until after five hours of work. So when I asked Kris for a break before the appointed time, she answered with an emphatic "No." Kris's message was clearly that we do our jobs by the book, no exceptions.

Over time at this Burger King I began to notice that Kris wasn't a taskmaster all the time. Sure, during busy times she was prone to exhort the staff to work faster. And she didn't tolerate leaning (remember, "If you've got time to lean, you've got time to clean"). But this attitude relaxed a bit during slower times, and it especially relaxed for the better workers like Daniel, Eric, and Craig, three of the fastest guns on the sandwich assembly board.

So who makes the best managers: men or women? In my

fast food experience, women win, hands down! Until my last job—that is, when I worked for James—I was prepared to make the sweeping statement that all my female managers were better than my best male managers. Women managers seemed better at guiding people through periods of self-doubt or at offering genuinely nurturing help. One female manager, when seeing me stooped over the front register, raised the screen by propping a phone book underneath it. This simple act of kindness took me a long way toward forgiving her managerial warts and toward accepting those of this particular job. Others built their alliances by treating me with tact. Consider the same scenario, changing only the manager's gender. Every store asked me what size uniform I needed. In both a McDonald's, run by a female manager, and a Wendy's, where my interaction was with a male assistant manager, I gave the same answer: 3X. Now I grant this is definitely a big boy size, but my McDonald's boss took this information in with no visible emotion, commenting only that she thought the shirt would be available in three to four days. When confronted with this same information, the Wendy's boss stared in consternation and said, "I don't think we have anything *that* big." He promised to check with the district manager, though, and said he would solve the problem. Here's how it was "solved": He simply went ahead and gave me the skin-tight XL that I had rejected earlier. I felt betrayed, tricked, and humiliated—working all day in front of coworkers and customers in a shirt that leaves none of my excesses to the imagination.

The Crew Members

But what about the people who work fast food? Most of the stores I worked in had 30 to 40 crew members, about half of them males, half females. Usually there were two or three workers over 45, but most were 30 or younger. Every store had a mix of nationalities. On the standard dimensions of diversity (age, nationality, and gender), fast food is a good corporate citizen. Beyond these obvious dimensions, though, if you work fast food long enough, four different types of crew members emerge, distinguished by why they work fast food.

The Survival Worker

Why fast food? I asked this question in a lot of different ways. More than once I was told, admittedly not in these words, that they didn't think they could do any better. They were simply struggling to survive and didn't have time to ask: "Can I do better?" Here are the profiles of three such workers.

PROFILE 1: MARSHA. Marsha was about 50 years old and worked the lobby at Burger King. This job was the easiest in the store: Greet customers when they came in and clean up after they left. Marsha resisted learning any other jobs. Reluctantly, she had learned how to wash dishes, but she resisted learning any other tasks. This attitude frustrated Kris, and she admitted to me in one candid moment that she was cutting Marsha's hours. It was midwinter, and customers were scarce. "We don't need a greeter," she told me. Each week Marsha's hours were cut until she was down to just Friday service, the busiest day of the week. I was off duty one day when I noticed Marsha was still sitting in the lobby even though her shift had been over for more than an hour. I decided to sit with her. At first she was wary, but she grew more relaxed as it became clear that I was truly interested in her story.

Marsha lived in a double-wide manufactured home with her mother and husband. They had one car for the three of them—hence, Marsha waited until her husband was off shift before he could pick her up and she could go home. Herb worked at a Sam's Club about three miles away. Having one car was a trade-off she gladly made since it allowed her to make payments on the home they had recently moved into. As we talked, Marsha admitted worrying. She didn't understand why she got so few hours, and she despaired of ever being able to get a second car. It was not my place to tell her this had been a conscious decision by Kris, that either she became more flexible in what she could do or she wouldn't get enough hours to survive. Kris was unyielding when it came to performance. Months later I went into the local

BJ's, a competitor of Sam's Club, and Marsha was the greeter there. I warmly said hello, but she didn't recognize me.

PROFILE 2: JULIE. When she was 18, Julie used to work at this Burger King, but she left when she got married. Now divorced, she had returned to the only thing she knew. She was on the first window taking customers' orders. She was chatty and in a good mood. Her brother had just agreed to sell her his old car. It had 175,000 miles on it, but she proudly announced it would be hers if she could come up with $700. She couldn't wait to own it, but she admitted she didn't know how she would meet the $50 per month payment her brother expected.

PROFILE 3: ANNA. Anna was a single mother. She was 21, a high school dropout, and had a newborn baby. At one point she told me she made $6.50 an hour and worked six hours a day. She wanted to know how much that was. Then she told me she paid $3 an hour for a babysitter. "How much is left over?" she asked. She was resigned to the answer. Working most of a day for $21 isn't a winning formula. I pressed her to try something else because other than her poor math skills, Anna was quite intelligent. I suggested she try getting her GED and then enrolling in junior college. She responded, "I've never had anyone encourage me." Maybe so, but it was clear this route wasn't working. When I suggested trying for some higher-paying job, Anna said she didn't have time to even breathe. I didn't think Anna was going to try changing her status any time soon.

The Way-Station Worker

Many crew members professed that fast food was just a stopping-off point where they were marking time until better things happened. Many in this category were high school students or even college students, earning money until the next stage in their lives could begin. Some were dreamers putting varying levels of effort into realizing a better life.

RANDY AND JACKIE. Randy had worked more than five years at Arby's. On weekends he played for a death-metal band. Randy was serious about his dream, and others on the crew acknowledged that he was good and perhaps on his way to success. Over the years the band slowly had built a following, and the gigs were seemingly getting better with time. Randy had a CD he offered to sell me for $6. I told him unless he sang like Martha and the Vandellas, I wasn't likely to appreciate his music. He laughed, clearly harboring an ego unfazed by an old guy's rejection. (I liked to joke with my fellow crew members and with customers and continued to find this the most fun part of the job.) Jackie, who had worked front counter with me, was home-schooled and had completed all the credits needed for graduation early. She was putting in time at this job until her class graduated, and then she intended to go off to cosmetology school. She

FROM BEHIND THE COUNTER

Andy at Arby's seems adrift. He is friendly enough, so I ask him how long he has worked at Arby's. At first he says nothing, and then he reluctantly admits that he's been here for two years. Though this seems to embarrass him, later he proudly boasts that he made $3,500 working here last year. It was mid-January in Buffalo—barely 19°F—and Andy rides his bike to work every day. When I ask him why, he says, "Because that's the only way I have to get here, man!"

bragged about how she had gotten $75 to cut and style someone's hair for the prom.

TAMMY. Tammy was a moody girl who put on a gruff exterior. When Amy told her she was too slow to work the first assembly station during lunch rush, Tammy asked to use the bathroom, and when she emerged, it was clear she'd been crying. I think the toughness was a cover-up for an insecure girl. While in a good mood, Tammy talked about how she was going to become a pilot. First, though, she was going to enlist in the Air Force or go to the Air Force Academy. I was reluctant to tell her about all the hurdles she would face, not the least of which was a five-foot-seven-inch frame that packed more than 250 pounds.

The Aimless Worker

I'm not sure if the Aimless Worker is just a subset of the Way-Station Worker, differentiated only by the realization that dreams don't always come true. Donna was a perfect example. She started work my second day at Burger King. Much to my surprise, her first job was taking orders at the drive-thru window. What gives? Newbies don't start on the window; it's too hard. When I struck up a conversation with her, she told me in a tired voice that this was her second stint at BK. She had a kid, and the bills had to be paid. This was a safe harbor that I suspected she would never leave.

Daniel was good at sandwich assembly, and Kris clearly valued him. He often worked eight-hour days and was very fast. How fast and well you could do the job was a badge of honor, and more hours would typically go to he who won the battle. This was a problem for Daniel, though, because more days than not, Kris asked him to work extra hours beyond those scheduled. Unless Kris was very persistent, Daniel would usually find a way to beg off.

Daniel lamented one day that he'd only gotten four hours of sleep the night before. He had been up till 2:30 a.m. trying to master a Play Station 2 game so he could beat his friend on it. He could beat his friend on every other Play Station game and didn't want to lose to him on this one. Here was a college graduate, at least 22 years old, who had worked at Burger King for 10 months. He professed no higher ambition.

FROM BEHIND THE COUNTER

Eric is a first assistant who, when he has to substitute temporarily as manager while Kris is out, proves to be either overwhelmed or just not as good as Kris. I snap at him twice and feel badly about it largely because my anger is really directed at Kyle, who is turning out to be a real pain. He is the longest-tenured person here but also the slowest assembler, so much so that others mock him behind his back.

I keep falling further and further behind on my job because Kyle continually asks me to do things he should be able to do himself.

When my wife calls twice in tears about the deteriorating health of her dad, I realize I will have to quit. When I get there and learn Kris isn't there, I tell Kyle, who listens dispassionately and says only two things: "Does Kris know about this?" and, clearly showing how little he cares about my plight, "Do you know how to fix printers when the cartridge isn't working right?"

The Career Worker

Fast food restaurants have clear promotion paths and encourage workers to strive for advancement. Like most organizations, though, the ladder is more like a pyramid than a rectangle. Stick around, be reliable, do the job reasonably, and you can make it to crew leader. Stick around even longer, and shift supervisor or assistant manager positions are within reach. Sometimes these jobs open up because of turnover, and the initial ascent is rapid. Ask Allen, the assistant manager at McDonald's in Michigan. He had been there only nine months, but he was fast and had good interpersonal skills. More importantly, though, turnover had left openings at the assistant manager level, and his talents were rewarded. It's possible to move quickly through the first levels of the management pyramid. But while there might be multiple shift supervisors and assistant managers, there's only one manager per store. Consequently, career progress beyond assistant manager is slow. Perhaps because of this, I saw the most dissatisfaction at the assistant manager level. Both Nicole at McDonald's and Orville at Wendy's were assistant managers. Both were exempt-status employees— extra hours of work weren't compensated with overtime pay. Both worked for managers who showed no signs of leaving and creating a promotion opportunity. Both showed signs of moving on.

It was common for store managers to have high seniority. The next level in the career path was district manager, supervising a string of stores, typically for a franchise owner. Even good managers found it hard to jump to district managers. There just weren't that many openings at the narrow part of the pyramid. Take the case of Kris at Burger King.

Kris was the best manager I had worked for, and she had

FROM BEHIND THE COUNTER

Nicole is the assistant manager at a McDonald's. I ask her out of curiosity how many hours the managers work; she is surprisingly open and tells me she wishes she hadn't taken the promotion to assistant manager because it meant that she is now salaried and gets no overtime for working more than 40 hours. She adds that most managers work 55 or more hours per week.

been with Burger King for 10 years. She lamented that her management job might be a dead end—not many district manager jobs were opening up in the local area. She had a husband and at least one young child, and working fifty-five hours or more per week made meeting family demands tough. Other workers, though, appeared stalled in their career progress, in part because no openings existed, but more likely because of personal deficiencies.

During a very busy, short-staffed day, Jeff and Orville had a loud and very unprofessional exchange, all in front of the customers, that began when Orville announced he was leaving without doing the customary general cleanup. Jeff had been stewing about the short-staff situation already, and this last bit from Orville pushed him over the edge. I figured out later on that much of this fight involved wages: Orville was an exempt employee and was not legally entitled to be paid overtime. Jeff, one level lower in the management chain, *did* receive overtime pay. With overtime, Jeff earned nearly the same amount as Orville—about $35,000. No wonder there was tension between the two.

One advantage of high turnover was that it created promotion opportunities. Good employees could advance from crew member to crew leader to shift supervisor fairly quickly, and the pay increases could be quite nice. Crew leaders generally made about a dollar more than new crew members. Part of this difference was probably due to time on the job. The big jump occurred from crew leader to shift supervisor. At the shift supervisor level, wages were about $11 per hour. And as we saw with Jeff, with time and a half for hours over 40, this could lead to a mid-$30s income, which was not terrible for a high school graduate not yet 30 years old. Things slowed down, though, at the assistant manager level. These were classified as exempt employees, so they weren't entitled to overtime pay. Working over 50 hours per week with significant managerial responsibilities seemed to wear heavily on the assistant managers I talked to.

As with any corporation, advancements were less frequent as you moved up the ladder. One store manager told me it takes about a decade to make store manager, and many assistants burn out long before that happens.

The rhythms and rituals of work are strange things. I've written elsewhere that employee motivation came from three sources.[2] First, a supervisor, through performance management practices, sets up a series of tasks and performance expectations. When this was done clearly, workers rose to the responsibility. Similarly, rewards and punishments shaped employee behavior. In my estimation, the rhythms and rituals of work—that is, the culture that was built up over time—had the strongest impact on what we did. While I've seen this in many companies where I've consulted, from high tech to no tech, nowhere was this more evident than in fast food. At my best Burger King, Kris made clear from the first day what was expected. So deeply ingrained in us were these expectations that even when Kris wasn't around, other workers would signal to newbies what was required. Sometimes these signals were blatant. Put the buns in the warmer tray backward, and the sandwich assembler stopped what she was doing and picked up the buns you had just misplaced and turned them around: "It's faster this way," she said simply. Sometimes the signals were more subtle. Remember the story of Marsha? She couldn't or wouldn't adapt to learning multiple jobs. Managers needed this. Flexibility was crucial. When workers quit or didn't show up—a common occurrence in fast food—having a crew who could quickly be shuffled into vacant jobs was essential. Marsha's hours kept being cut. Every store I worked in had some chart, usually visibly posted for all to see, that indicated the major tasks and who could perform them. Gold stars were placed in a cell when a worker learned a task.

---

2 George Milkovich and Jerry Newman, *Compensation*, 8th ed. (New York: McGraw-Hill/Irwin, 2003).

Lunch Rush

The rhythms and rituals tell people what they're supposed to do and when. In strong cultures these rhythms and rituals actually make life easier. Even when the manager isn't watching, or maybe isn't on site, you know what to do. Accordingly, good companies build strong cultures. They send clear messages that are unwaveringly transmitted down the pyramid by managers who believe in the content of those messages and who through word and deed indicate what is expected. So powerful are these messages that even in situations where no explicit rule exists, or where you don't have time to think about the governing rule, you almost instinctually know the right way to proceed.

Nowhere in fast food is this more evident than at lunch rush. When you don't have time to ask questions, knowing what is coming is comforting. For example, I quickly found that lunch rush was no time to ask for a bathroom break. Oh, you can ask. And it will be granted. But the air of disapproval is evident. Next time you wait.

Store managers schedule many part-timers to begin a shift just before mealtime as a way of keeping costs down. Every day there is one insane period: the aforementioned LUNCH RUSH. Rules change during lunch rush: Social conventions disappear, and the pace of work life moves into overdrive. People come to fast food restaurants because they want their food *fast*. This creates expectations from customers and magnifies the importance of moving quickly for workers. Consequently, every store has strict time standards: Cash registers double as computers, keeping track of when orders are placed and when they are filled.

Store managers who regularly missed deadlines weren't store managers for long, and all these pressures rolled downhill. Every worker took lunch rush seriously. I don't think I ever worked a lunch rush where people didn't regularly run—not walk—from task to task. And with a fine sheen of grease coating the floor most times, this wasn't easy. And I don't think I ever worked a lunch rush where someone didn't yell or snap at someone else. The pressures of getting food out immediately shattered polite social rules. Just as quickly as it started, lunch rush was over. Temper flare-ups were forgotten when the pace slowed. Sometimes the insanity lasted little more than an hour, but sometimes it extended almost until dinnertime.

I was amazed at my first lunch rush, an experience at Wendy's that lasted from 11:30 a.m. until almost 2 p.m. One minute there were three people ordering food inside and a couple of cars lined up outside. The next minute the line was out the door and takeout customers were wrapped around the building. As if we didn't know this, the manager would bark out the battle cry: "Customers are out the door, people. Let's get moving!" And move we did. Sandwiches were slapped together, pickles sometimes askew, ketchup perhaps leaking out the side of a sandwich that an hour ago might not have passed inspection. Fries disappeared from the warming bin as quickly as you made them, even with four baskets cooking at once. The manager yelled to pull the fries, even though they were 30 seconds away from being done. A special sandwich wasn't made as instructed. The runner angrily yelled to the assembler, "This has *mayo!* Make a new one!" The assembler, in the quest for speed, tried to wipe off the mayo. It didn't work. He tossed the burger toward the trash can specially designated for "mistakes" (used to inventory waste and audit possible theft) and missed the can. No one picked up the mess that resulted—it would have to wait until after rush. Cursing his errant throw, the assembler, already working at top speed, somehow mustered an extra burst of speed—the runner was watching and impatiently waiting. The order was filled, but now the overhead computer screen showed an even larger backlog. A big man came to the front counter and ordered 15 cheeseburgers. The counter worker took the order pleasantly, but the news brought silent groans from the assembly crew. Someone yelled, no one paid attention to whom, "Get Don up here, now!" Don had been working utility—whatever anyone needed, he got or did. Don, though, was in the big refrigerator, pulling up more burgers, so he didn't hear the command, and no one could see him. It didn't even occur to anyone to leave their station to go hunting—the first commandment shall never be broken: Serve the customer fast. The anonymous yeller tried again, this time more frantically, "Where the hell is Don? We need him!" Don emerged with a case of burgers and was about to put them in the holding refrigerator up front, but when he heard the yelling, he dropped the burger box on the floor, where it remained another obstacle until the rush was over. Don was needed on the assembly board, and that took precedence over everything else.

I raised my head to look at the clock, sweat dripping down my face, and was amazed that almost two hours had passed. Even the clock seemed to have obeyed the commands to move faster. Collectively, we realized the rush was over. The flood of orders had subsided to a trickle. Where four people had been working feverishly making sandwiches, now only two were needed. Not sure yet whether this was a real end or only a brief intermission, the remaining people began stocking supplies and doing some quick housekeeping. The burger on the floor was picked up and the area mopped. Don's dropped box of burgers was opened and its contents dumped into the holding refrigerator. Lettuce bins were filled, tomatoes were replenished, rolls and burgers continued to be cooked, and inventories were replenished. Everyone stood ready to meet another rush, but it didn't come. Not a word was said about the heroic efforts to get the food out. It was expected. This is fast food, people!

There wasn't much time for fun during the lunch rush.

Before and after, though, you threw some young kids together and they would find a way to entertain themselves, especially

FROM BEHIND THE COUNTER

I face a battle in what I'm now calling the "Great Cheese Wars." A coworker sees I'm getting to know the fry station but clearly wants to show who is boss. At one point two fry buzzers go off at the same time. Weighing in at less than 100 pounds and measuring five feet two inches at most, she lifts both fry baskets out of the oil at the same time and in one practiced motion lands them on the draining bar. Barely a drop of excess oil falls before she hoists the baskets again, inverting them in a perfectly timed arc that ends with fries nestled in their warming bins. For her size this is a dangerous action, but she executes it to perfection. Without even looking back, she strides to the front counter, somehow knowing that I'm watching in awe. Girls 1, old guy 0.

when the manager was not around. The favorite pastime was throwing objects at each other, like Hacky Sacks smuggled on the job or dodgeball pickles. Hit your target and you were regaled with cheers. If the pickle was caught, though, be prepared for grief. Even knives. One particularly deranged worker feinted at throwing a sharp knife at a friend. Other times the entertainment was hilarious. There was no shortage of intelligent people working fast food, and when there was time to entertain each other, no shortage of talent existed.

* * *

Some of the games weren't nearly as much fun. Several of the jobs I worked at involved personal challenges. I was the new guy, and there was always someone who assumed the job of letting me know this.

I was finally getting the hang of assembling sandwiches at a McDonald's when we got three orders for a total of 12 cheeseburgers. Then this thin wiry guy came back and took a place on the assembly board in front of me. Others had done this too, but they followed McDonald's assembly line procedures—I got the roll, put the meat on it, and passed it along to the next person for completion. But this guy was different. He motioned to me to make my own cheeseburgers and he would make his. Unusual, I thought, but okay. He waited, poised to start. I was wondering why he wasn't making sandwiches when he motioned to me to begin. It dawned on me that he was waiting until I made the first move! Something in his form, hunched over the assembly board, watching my hands, conjured up the old Wild West gunfights. I bit. With a flurry of motion I started my first burger, tenths of seconds ahead of him. But it was clear his technique was better, not to mention that his reflexes were quicker. By the time he finished his first three, I was still trying to wrap my second. He finished another three before I could begin to wrap my fourth. Disdaining helping me finish the task, he walked away. He had won this battle in the Great Cheese Wars. Despite myself, I felt lessened.

FROM BEHIND THE COUNTER

I overhear a roofer talking to his buddy about having to work overtime this afternoon, and the temperature is in the high 80s, probably 15 degrees hotter on a roof. I pop up and say something like "Such egregious treatment shouldn't go unpunished." The roofers say nothing, maybe because a McDonald's employee's view of the world is irrelevant to them, or maybe they got stuck on "egregious." But I'm overheard by a man in a suit who turns out to be a VP of sales for a local company. He asks me how long I've worked here. When I tell him just a short period, he asks what I did before. When I tell him I was a college teacher, my standard answer in this situation, he says that explains it, and gratuitously adds that I'm too good for this job. Mentally I disagree with him. I've found many bright, hardworking people working in fast food. Seldom are they told this.

Other wars were more good-natured. A favorite I was told about but did not witness emulated chugging contests, but in this chugging contest the shake machine was the center of attention. All you had to do was place your head under the spigot while a coworker pulled back the handle. A steady stream of shake more than a half-inch thick in diameter would then flow into the mouth, and either brain freeze or an overflowing mouth would make short work of even the most determined contestant. I suspected the game wasn't to see who lasted the longest but rather to have a riotous laugh as shake spilled out of the player's mouth and onto his face and clothes.

Fast food isn't a high-prestige occupation. Anyone who watches television or movies sees fast food workers portrayed negatively as burned-out, never-has-beens, jokesters more intent on the next yuk than the next customer, or even as workers trying to hide their job identity because the nice-looking girl working at the Gap on the far end of the mall might look down on them. Or worse yet, they're invisible.

* * *

How do you keep a positive image of yourself when the
work you do is socially assaulted by well-meaning friends or colleagues? I saw two intelligent responses to shelter young egos. The first was to create an insular group: Make your friendships within crews and interact primarily with people facing the same status assaults, and the fortification can protect you. It was very common to have off-duty workers hanging around, talking to crew on break or even mingling behind the counter. They chose their times well, knowing such behavior wouldn't be tolerated during rush. Even in nonrush periods, though, some managers didn't like such bonding. My Arby's experience included a hard-and-fast rule: When you're off duty, you're not there unless it's to buy food. In contrast, some of the best managers in other places I worked encouraged the opposite behaviors. At my first

Burger King, it wasn't uncommon for workers to drop by and say hello. Kris, the store manager, even set up evening social events to encourage crew friendships. If your best friends work with you, a community of like-minded people evolves. I met a worker at Wendy's who came in to talk with friends even months after quitting the job.

The second way fast food workers distanced themselves from negative perceptions of the work had to do with the way the crews were organized. There was a very rigid hierarchy in fast food based strictly on job difficulty and mastery. I found the hardest jobs to be the drive-thru window and assembler. When lunch rush started, you saw the natural ordering: The fittest took their places at the jobs demanding the most talent, and these people were duly rewarded. The cherished prize of more hours usually went to these folks who could master the hardest jobs and thrive even during lunch rush. Daniel, an assembler at Burger King, always assumed first board position when the rush came. This was the pilot of the back operations. Looking at the computer screen, he would delegate jobs almost instantly. Second assembly, located on the opposite side of the condiments and warming bins, received orders from Daniel: "I need four Whoppers, no onions," he would shout. Second assembly rushed to the task. "We're low on Angus!" and I immediately dropped everything and headed for the freezer. In answer to the question, "Where's the beef?" It's always in the back cooler.

Even Daniel, who got more hours than he wanted (and creatively found ways to turn down additional hours), had superiors. Yes, some of them had higher ranks, but status in fast food was most often based on job proficiency. Daniel reluctantly admitted that three people were faster assemblers than he was. Unable to figure out why he wasn't faster, he resigned himself to second-tier status. But he was faster than most, so he was almost content.

On the wall in several stores, or located prominently on a manager's desk, were charts showing crew members' proficiencies. Master a task and a gold star was affixed in a box next to your name. Master all the tasks and there was a row of stars sufficient to make any general envious. When I first saw these charts, I mentally noted that most everyone could do more than I could. I was at the bottom of a hierarchy, even an intentionally insulated one.

4

Will Work for Whoppers!

Kris, whom you met in the last several chapters, specifically stated that hiring people who fit in was her major goal. When I left this job some weeks later, citing serious family illness (true), she was visibly disappointed. In one of the few compliments I received during my 14 months undercover, she told me I fit in well with the people there and that she would miss me. She had worked hard to create fit. She had spent one hour interviewing me, whereas others had completed that chore in five minutes or so. My first day at work I noted a bulletin board with candid pictures of all the crew members in off-duty situations. She admitted to organizing social outings, the most recent of which had been a bowling social. Kris spent time during work hours connecting with employees as well, particularly those who were good workers, and she dedicated much of her time to creating and maintaining a unified harmonious culture.

James, my manager at Krystal, believed in a cohesive culture as well, which he built with humor. I learned that he had this personality trait during my job interview. Under the section on the employment application that asked why I wanted this job, I had prefaced my comments by saying, "You probably think I'm crazy, but. . . ." James then started

the interview, shouting from 10 feet away as he began walking toward me, "Yes, you must be crazy!" I came to discover
in my short stint at Krystal that James had a group of people
who loved to rag on each other. On my first day the other
crew members took turns poking fun at James and his work
schedule. There was very little overlap between his time off
and the schedule of his wife, who worked as the manager at
a rival fast food restaurant. Stories about what she would do
in her spare time while he pulled 24-hour shifts led to fits
of laughter, which he took with good-natured cheer. Since
I have a bit of sarcasm in my soul too, I quickly joined in the
repartee. James had hired an individual who he thought
would fit into this environment.

Both Kris and James worked hard to learn about each of
their employees, and they made sure everyone knew each
other as well, whether through on-site bull sessions or social
activities outside of work. In doing so, they sent the message
that each employee was worthy of respect and was part of a
team.

And then there was Kristen, at the opposite end of the
spectrum. At this particular restaurant, fit was never a priority. In fact, to me, the store seemed to be divided into two
camps, both equally strong and separated by language barriers. Everyone on the sandwich assembly crew was Hispanic,
and there was only one translator who spoke more than a
few words of English. All the remaining staff members
spoke English. As best as I could tell, neither group intentionally disrespected the other, but there were clear signs of
barriers that made the workplace uncomfortable.

Crew members on the front-end jobs were absolutely dependent on sandwich assemblers. When sandwiches were slow to arrive, customers got cranky. It was exponential: Very slow equaled exceedingly cranky. If a sandwich was made incorrectly by the assemblers, the front end took the verbal abuse. Last-minute order changes by a customer were easier to communicate with a few spoken words than with written messages sent by the computer-register. But when the assemblers spoke little English, anything beyond "no mayo on this Whopper" frequently was met with blank stares. And in the heat of lunch rush, if an order change was yelled to the back assembly area rather than politely called out, the language wall became impenetrable. All of these realities meant the two groups had to get along with each other and talk to each other. Kristen had the opportunity to intervene, much as Kris and James did in their restaurants. But she didn't understand the concept of "fit." In fact, this was the only store where I wasn't interviewed at all. A phone call the night before I was scheduled to report was the only advance conversation I had. Failing to hire for fit, perhaps saving time in the early stages of employment, comes back to haunt managers later on.

Wouldn't it have been embarrassing if, after all my

planning, I couldn't get a job? Well, as I described earlier, it took longer than I had anticipated to land my first one. Through this experience, I realized how uniform the questions were on the job applications across the restaurants I applied at: What hours do you want to work? Do you have reliable transportation? What days do you want to work? But what was handled very differently was the interview process. It seemed that some of the managers, like Kris and James, had a strong sense of the team they wanted to create and where they fit on that team. All the talk in management books about vision and leadership begins in the hiring decisions, and great managers don't minimize this first step. Several of my managers never learned this lesson—most of my interviews lasted less than 10 minutes. In one extreme case, the manager at a store in Michigan saw my application, called me on the phone, and told me I would start work the following day with no interview whatsoever. In two stores I was hired as soon as the manager realized that the hours I was willing to work fit with the store's needs. Both interviews lasted less than two minutes. Only two stores gave me more extensive interviews. I'm convinced part of the reason these were among the best places I worked was that the managers knew the importance of hiring workers who fit into the existing culture.

Kris was different from any other manager I had faced.

I was expecting another five-minute interview, but she kept me for an hour. The questions were designed to find out what kind of person I was. In fact, I learned during the interview that Kris wanted to hire someone who would fit in with the group of people she already had working for her. She was proud of the crew she had assembled, and she wanted to make sure the good chemistry was left intact. Her turnover rate, she proudly announced, was 111 percent—remarkable in an industry known for rates more than double this.

The interview itself was definitely not the typical line of questions I had experienced previously. Kris asked about my teaching: Where did I teach? What did I teach? How did I feel about teaching? And then the hard ball, "We've hired teachers before, and they had problems with colleagues or students coming in as customers, and our teachers seemed to be embarrassed at being caught working fast food. How would you handle that?" At the time I laughed. Clearly she didn't know me. I had bragged in class that I was going to work fast food. I told her this, and she clearly liked the answer.

From the first minute, Kris sent the message that this was not some second-class job for which she was hiring a third-class citizen. Her first role as a leader was to make sure I understood what I was getting into and what was expected of me in *her* store. One of her key questions alerted me to the job pressures I would face—pressures that were often glossed over by other managers intent on filling positions immediately. Kris asked how I would handle working in pressured conditions, with unhappy customers lining up during the lunch rush. Fortunately, I had supervised a concession stand staff that had managed to survive a high school state championship where lines were regularly 20 people or more deep, with everyone clamoring for fast service before the next game started. That I understood the stress this created and still came back for more reassured Kris. Lots of yelling and lots of pressure to get food out quickly are regular parts of the fast food job. Kris knew that the ability to deal with this was a key requirement, and even if it took hours to find just the right person, she was willing to invest that time.

* * *

I had dropped my application off with James, the store
manager, around midmorning. Without looking at it, he told me to come back that afternoon and he would interview me. When I arrived, James wasn't on the premises, and I later learned that he had left to pick up a worker who had no other way of getting there for his shift. When he arrived, James immediately apologized for making me wait. His second words were, as I mentioned above, "Are you crazy?" And we were off to the races. Before I could answer affirmatively, he said, "I knew something strange was going on when I saw you made $1.65 in your last fast food job." He had actually read through the whole application. I'd had no sign prior to this, now my seventh job, that anyone (other than Kris) had read the application, but he noticed that back in 1968 and 1969 I had worked as a short-order cook, then night supervisor, at Crazy Jim's Blimpy Burgers in Ann Arbor, Michigan. James and his colleagues relied on good-natured ribbing to keep the group collegial, and as if to signal that, he said, "And I saw when you worked that job. That's 10 years before I was born!" Thanks, James. But that was before I knew him well enough to know that he was *including* me. Ultimately, I found James to be very polite and a potentially gifted leader.

During our interview, James focused on why I wanted the job. I told him my wife was sick of my hanging around the house all day, and I had decided to make her happy and at the same time satisfy a long love affair with cooking fast food. I launched into a couple of stories about cooking for large crowds at the sports complex and supervising people who weren't sure that they wanted to do this kind of work. I could tell he liked me when he shared stories about the lengths to which he has had to go to get people at work and on time.

There are literally dozens of general selection tools available for finding new employees, but fast food stores don't use any of them except applications and interviews. I was never asked to take a physical. I guess if I couldn't do the job, I was gone. I was never drug tested. Show signs of drug use, you were fired. Be involved in an accident, then you were screened for drugs. Fail and you were fired. Similarly, if you started showing up for work hung over, eventually it would cost you your job. One Wendy's employee regularly came in to work clearly hung over. The manager put up with this for a while largely because the kid (he looked to be barely old enough to drink milk, let alone alcohol) at least showed up even though it was clear he didn't feel much like working. After 3 days of this over a 10-day period, the store manager gave him an ultimatum: Come in ready to work or you're done. I never saw the kid again.

Fast food stores needed to figure out which applicants

really wanted a job and were willing to work. Excessive

turnover occurred because managers typically hired people and then just waited to see who would stick. Within two or three weeks the poorly performing applicants were fired or they quit—that is, they didn't show up. Applicant histories indicated whether an employee who had previously quit had given any notice. Those who had given prior notice were frequently hired back if they reapplied later. Those who had not done so had committed a cardinal sin in fast food and were put on do-not-hire lists that circulated among stores in the local area. One way to figure out who was willing to go the extra distance and who was motivated to work would have been to make the selection process more onerous. Consider first the way my Wendy's and McDonald's jobs unfolded. Then let me describe a different scenario that might have weeded out applicants who lacked the motivation to stick with a fast food job.

On my first day working at Wendy's, I was deluged with training materials that, I was informed very curtly, I was expected to learn very quickly. Similarly, at a McDonald's in New York, I had to learn how to make 13 sandwiches for which the ingredients included 4 types of buns, 9 main ingredients (chicken and hamburger variations), and 12 condiments. Thank goodness all the different combinations of these three categories of ingredients weren't available to customers. As I was writing this, two of our best statisticians at SUNY Buffalo were figuring out the number of combinations possible. I suggested we go to McDonald's and order just one of each type of sandwich and count up the possible combinations. When Professors Orange and Krzystofiak told me the total was 147,456 combinations, my next suggestion was: Get fries with that.

In reality each of the 13 sandwiches had a specific bun, meat, and condiment package. In fact, all the fast foods had very specific orders of assembly. The whole process was daunting for new crew members, particularly with time pressures from customers. To circumvent the system, I asked if I could take home the ingredients list and memorize it on my own. While this earned me brownie points, it also got me several resounding "No's." Either they didn't have the list readily available, or they wanted employees to learn it as part of the paid work of the job. My suggestion for both Wendy's and McDonald's: Make some or all of this training part of the prehiring selection process. A person applies for a job, and management is interested in hiring the person based on the application. The manager asks the applicant to come in to schedule an interview. When the applicant comes in to schedule the interview, the manager gives him or her a sandwich chart that the applicant must learn and be tested on at the interview. While I can't guarantee this would cut out those who lack motivation, I do know it would narrow the pool of applicants and help reduce turnover.

* * *

My wages for the seven fast food jobs never exceeded

$6.50 per hour. Maybe I could have earned more if I had haggled, but I decided early on that I wouldn't argue for a higher wage. I reasoned that most kids who worked fast food wouldn't have the skills or confidence to try negotiating for more money. Only once did I deviate from this strategy. At one job the store manager interviewed me and offered $5.15 per hour.[1] I thought the minimum wage was $5.35 per hour and said so—after all, I'm a human resources professor and coauthor of a book on compensation—surely I knew the minimum wage. (When I got home and looked up the minimum, I was totally embarrassed by my glaring error.) The manager mistook my stupidity for a negotiating ploy. She immediately said she would try to push for $5.50 an hour. I was not overly impressed since all my other jobs paid either $6.25 or $6.50.

This brings up a critical question: How can a fast food

store survive while paying a dollar less than the competition, particularly when the competition is no more than a mile or two down the road? Economists would say it's not *rational* for people to take $5.15 or $5.50 when they can travel a mile and make $6.50 doing what is basically the same job. Does that make fast food workers *irrational?* How did these restaurants succeed with less than two miles separating them? Two, from the same national chain and within five miles of each other, paid wages differing by more than 20 percent.

There are three possible explanations. First, the stores paying at the low end did so because they could! It's one

---

1 I won't mention the name of the restaurant to protect an unusually candid store manager.

thing to say the stores were only a mile or so apart. It's quite another to figure out how to get to the more distant store. I saw kids getting to work by every imaginable means of loco-motion except chariots: in new cars that put my clunker to shame; in old cars; in cars driven by relatives, boyfriends, or girlfriends; on foot; on buses; on bicycles; and on roller blades. All but the first of these transport sources can be un-reliable. And if there is a big labor market of kids willing to work for the lower wage because they have no easy way to get to the higher-paying jobs, then the stores take advantage of it. I also don't think it's any huge coincidence that the low-paying stores I experienced either straddled or were in the heart of low-income neighborhoods.

Second, despite what Thomas Jefferson said, all men aren't created equal, at least when it comes to working fast food. Low-paying stores could survive by hiring people who couldn't get work, or remain working, elsewhere. Example: Michelle, the worker at Krystal who was characterized as bipolar by crew members. One minute she would be work-ing hard, the next she was tattling on a coworker or trying to foist off a hard job on someone else. Or Elaine, who had been fired by two other Wendy's stores and was now at this third one only because of her friendship with the manager. I wasn't there a week when Elaine took a can of aerosol veg-etable spray and set it on fire with a lighter. She laughed hysterically as flames shot out about two feet. No manager saw her that time, and they continued to put up with her other odd behavior because she was very good at her job when motivated, and it was difficult to attract good workers to these low-wage jobs.

Good managers were amazingly tolerant of a worker's idiosyncrasies. Show up on time, do the job well, and behavioral quirks were tolerated. But good managers also made it clear where the boundaries were. Frequently the boundaries involved other employees or safety. Frankie tolerated Ron's strange views of humor but reprimanded him when he propped the back door open to make multiple trips to the dumpster—a number of robberies in the local area had made such "minor violations" of safety procedures intolerable.

My final theory is a combo plate. Some workers were simply clueless. It took them a while to realize that other jobs paid better. And until they overcame their inertia, they stayed where they were. The staying part was the challenge. Good managers made jobs fulfilling in ways outside of the monetary rewards. For example, they set flexible hours. In one store, all I had to do was tell the manager how many total hours, how many per day, and what days I wanted to work, and the manager fed that data into a computer program that figured things out. And I appreciated being able to name my own hours. Places that were more accommodating were more desirable.

There are numerous rewards organizations can rely on when monetary incentives aren't an option. Fast food relies on the promise of social interaction, vacation time, and potential advancement, among others. However, I found that the most effective nonmonetary incentives were timely

FROM BEHIND THE COUNTER

Flamethrowers and alligators—it's just another day in the trenches. I already told you about the Wendy's employee who lit a vegetable spray and created an instant mini-flamethrower. She also liked to throw things—pickles, plastic forks, and once a knife used to cut salad vegetables. Funny stuff, that. No one ever caught her, even though she wasn't particularly secretive in her escapades.

More interesting is the day I am assigned to follow Ron around outside my Florida Wendy's job and learn how to police the area. Ron is a senior citizen over 70 years old who works because he has to. He's a hard worker, but he has a strange mix of obsessive-compulsive behaviors and peculiar humor that makes him much harder to appreciate.

feedback and recognition. Here's a listing of what managers do to encourage crew members to sometimes literally "work for Whoppers."

Because fast food is heavily populated by young people, vacation is a benefit that appeals to them, even though it is usually unpaid. Other benefits are less important. This group is notorious for thinking the spring in their step is an entitlement that will last forever. They don't want health care. They don't want a pension. Give them money and give them time off to spend it. For the most part fast food stores

I'm not sure how much skill there is to sweeping cigarette butts into a dustpan, but Ron takes his job very seriously, giving step-by-step detailed instructions. When we finish the paved area, Ron proceeds to tell me we need to check around the pond that is adjacent to the drive-thru area. As we walk toward the pond and Ron is inspecting for any signs of litter, he stops and reports: "It doesn't look like we need to go around the pond today, but if you ever have to do this job by yourself, be on the lookout for alligators." My first reaction is disbelief, and I look quickly at his face for any signs that a practical joke is afoot. Nothing. I tell him I am not being paid enough to go alligator hunting. He cackles and says that maybe I don't get to choose what happens on this job. Fortunately, I quit three days later, without being asked to police the "alligator swamp."

seemed to accommodate this attitude very well. A few of the stores offered health insurance, but it didn't kick in until after three to six months of work. If you maintained twenty-five or more hours of work each week for an entire year at one Burger King, you were given one week of paid vacation. And to be truthful, those who work at fast food restaurants don't expect to receive good benefits—so much so that even many managers I worked for didn't know the basic information about what employees were entitled to. Only one of the managers I worked for gave information about benefits as part of the job interview. The most frequent response to questions about benefits that I got from other managers was "I don't know." Another perk important to fast food employees is the discount given on food. The lowest-paying store I worked at had the most liberal policy—any day, any time I could buy up to $15 worth of food at a discount of 50 percent. This was important to the kids, but it was a short-lived incentive. After a while, even the most robust eaters tended to tire of the fast food fare.

Social interactions became a key motivator for engaging the crew. In the last chapter you learned how Kris used culture to drive performance, productivity, and loyalty to the job. Encouraging team unity both inside and outside of the work environment clearly takes some thought and introspection, and Kris's success in this area was one of the reasons why I felt she was a strong manager. While she wasn't as naturally gifted as James, she clearly spent time thinking about how to improve her business and sustain those elements that drove success in fast food. It made me wonder how other managers could fall so short in this area.

And of course part of what leads patrons to return regularly to a particular location is customer satisfaction. Yes, they want their sandwiches assembled correctly, but it helps to have a welcoming atmosphere. Stores that intentionally cultivated teamwork—like Krystal with James as manager—also encouraged employees to interact with customers. In fact, this became one of my favorite things about working fast food: the chance to interact with customers beyond the highly scripted exchange. Maybe when you do it hundreds of times per week, hundreds of weeks in your life, the fun wears off. But I liked to personalize the fast food experience, and I thought it might make a difference. At Krystal, James made a conscious effort to create a bond with customers. Waitresses and waiters do this all the time in restaurants higher on the food chain, but fast food places are less inclined to. I think James knew that his product wasn't going to win the taste battle, and to keep customers coming back, he set up Bingo matches for Tuesday mornings, a traditionally slow time. He also emphasized that we should remember repeat customers and find ways to interact with them. I thrived on this kind of interaction.

※　　※　　※

The one reward employees can count on in fast food is

job security. Fast food places don't like to fire people. Too many quit as it is, without adding to turnover numbers and the recruitment problem. Sometimes, however, an employee will get fired. It appears that the one certain way to get fired is to behave unreliably. "Being reliable" means four things:

1. Coming to work

2. Being on time for work

3. Being in shape to work

4. Giving advance notice for necessary absences

Depending on the store, there was either zero or little tolerance for not abiding by these behavioral standards. Those standards, however, were fairly easy for most employees to meet. Furthermore, the tolerance level was often linked to how much they needed you. Good maintenance workers were hard to come by. At my McDonald's in Michigan, Miguel, the maintenance guy, had walked out in the middle of a shift several times without any explanation or advance notice. All of these incidents were attributed to a hair-trigger temper set off by disagreements with coworkers. Each time he came back the following day; each time he was forgiven.

I suspect it's possible to lose a job for poor performance, blatant safety violations, or insubordination, but on the whole I found managers and supervisors awfully tolerant of the antics of kids. They even gave me a reprieve. Fast food restaurants wanted people to do what they were told, when they were told to do it. Army discipline and assembly-line efficiency provided appropriate models. Because most employees were young, the stores tended to get people who hadn't learned how to challenge authority yet. Or perhaps they had expended all their authority challenges on hapless parents. Unlike this group, I came from an environment where challenges to the status quo were rewarded with academic tenure—essentially a promise of lifelong employment. This attitude carried over into my fast food jobs and tended to get me into trouble. I kept asking "why" on countless occasions, which didn't make my bosses happy, but neither did it get me fired. I decided that managers accepted a great deal from employees who were reliable and hardworking.

FROM BEHIND THE COUNTER

On one occasion, two preteen sisters come in with their parents. They buy their food in stages, three to be exact. For the main course the parents order. The next time only the two sisters come up. To make conversation, I ask the older sister if she likes her younger sibling. Without hesitating, she says no, emphatically. The look on her sister's face is heartbreaking. To hide her hurt, she too says no. But it's clear she would say yes if her sister said yes too. Later the younger one comes back alone to order two sundaes, and I give her a heaping mound of extra hot fudge, telling her to take that one because even if her sister is being mean, I think she is nice. She beams and makes my day.

Besides the value of job security, an incentive used successfully by fast food stores was the currency of hours on the job. Managers used this currency to encourage some employees and discourage others. While managers preferred not to fire crew members outright for unreliability or performing poorly, they indicated their disapproval of an employee's behavior by reducing that person' s hours until the individual couldn't afford to work there any longer and quit. Yes, it was passive-aggressive, I know—but in my experience passive-aggressive behavior is a common way of communicating by managers in many organizations around the country.

Moreover, driving an employee to quit by cutting his or her hours served a practical purpose: In most states, if you quit, you don't qualify for unemployment insurance.[2] Work hour assignments were also used to discipline. Freddy was an Arby's crew member whose dictionary included only four-letter words, but he was creative in using them as nouns, verbs, adjectives, and adverbs. And when he was excited, he didn't care who heard him conjugate his verbs, so to speak, customers included. The first time I heard Freddy cross the line, our manager Don said threateningly, "The next time a customer can hear you swearing, I will cut your hours to nothing." Hours also were used as rewards. So much so that those employees awarded extra hours often had to invent excuses why they couldn't regularly take on the additional time. I never had that problem—the learning curve on most jobs that matter to management was longer than I usually stayed at any one location.

The opportunity to experience different tasks was also used by management to motivate employees. In fact, if you like variety in your work, fast food might be the place for you. Granted, after you learn all the jobs, a certain monotony does set in. As I described earlier, there are seven distinct jobs in fast food. And store managers place a premium on learning all of them. Every store I worked in made it a practice to prominently post a sheet with everyone's name cross referenced by the jobs each had mastered. Each category had a gold or silver star indicating one's level of proficiency.

---

2 There are numerous exceptions to this blanket statement.

The more staff with interchangeable skills, the more flexible the entire operation.

Also, developing competencies across the crew lessened the harm caused by understaffing. In the never-ending quest to keep costs down, managers had huge incentives to keep the crew lean. Most stores I worked at regularly understaffed. Sometimes this was accidental—an employee called in was unavailable or quit before a shift unexpectedly—but more often a cost-conscious manager chose to get by with less help than needed.

Those workers who had aspirations to learn and advance were duly rewarded. Not only was there an opportunity to build new skills in fast food, there was an expectation that this would happen. Ideally, managers would be happiest if everyone could do every job. There was no direct wage increase for this skill-based diversity, but it seemed that those who thrived with new skills got more hours and were more likely to advance. The only roadblocks to development were personal ability and inclination. Some workers were content learning only a few jobs, and they resisted efforts to overcome this predilection. Other workers had skill sets narrowed by ability limits. Working the window required both easy-to-understand diction and ability to hear. The latter requirement may seem frivolous, but even with headphones it was not uncommon to have drive-thru crew members ask customers to repeat their orders. Wendy's required me to wear headphones while I worked as cook. Supposedly when a large order came in, this would give me a jump on loading the grill. This may have been true, but I could seldom understand the orders, particularly when the customers spoke with strong southern accents.

The promise of advancement is a motivating factor in any organization, and since every operation within a fast food chain basically has the same organizational structure, there is an opportunity to advance despite working in a variety of locations. The hierarchy is from bottom up: crew member, crew leader, shift supervisor, assistant manager (possible two or three levels of these), manager, and district manager. Moving up is based on time in job and performance.

The length of time until promotion depended heavily on opportunity. I saw an assistant manager at McDonald's who had made it to that position in less than one year. I saw other stores where such a move took several years. My first BK manager told me I could move up, but at the store manager level there was quite a glut, and moves into that job took a long time. The lower-level moves were accompanied by small hourly promotion pay increases, reported to me by some who had risen to those levels to be 15 to 25 cents per hour.

At Wendy's I hinted at interest in working my way into management just to see what would happen in terms of my relationships with the crew and managers. First, I was treated better. Jeff, the shift supervisor who hadn't spoken to me other than the occasional perfunctory hello, now took the time to show me pictures of a wedding ring and honeymoon site planned for his future bride. Second, I was privy to more information. Shift supervisors made low to mid-$20s plus overtime pay after 40 hours. Assistant managers made mid-$30s, and store managers made mid-$40s. Neither of these latter two groups got overtime. This was significant because working over 50 hours per week was very common for managers. Some of the more "A type" managers worked 70 hours regularly. A shift supervisor who got about 10 hours per week of overtime could easily earn pay equal to that of an assistant manager (500 extra hours per year at 1.5 times wages, or about $18, equals $9,000 extra). Remember Nicole, the assistant manager at a McDonald's who admitted to me that she had erred in taking the assistant manager's job? Turns out she was making less than she had when her job qualified her for overtime.[3]

✳ ✳ ✳

My research strongly suggests that recognition for a job well done is highly valued as a reward by employees. The better fast food managers long ago learned that recognition is inexpensive and powerful. Low-cost operations, something every global competitor strives for today, could learn a lesson from James at Krystal. Three times in my first days, the moments when taking such a job seems like idiocy and a good pick-me-up is in order, he told me I was doing a first-rate job. My second morning, after a sleepless night punctuated by increasing back pains, I was beginning to wonder if training as cook was a smart move. James countered with just the right recognition: "Jerry, I talked with some of the folks last night. They tell me you're doing a great job. I appreciate

---

3 The Fair Labor Standards Act requires payment of 1.5 times wages for hours over 40 in any week for workers not classified as management. Shift supervisors were not considered management.

the way you're developing as a cook." Bad leadership can't be passed off by bribing workers to stay and work hard with more money. Certainly the pain in my back couldn't be lessened by a few cents more in wages. But the recognition— well, I was just as susceptible as the next crew member. I've never seen a sincere compliment that didn't have a positive impact. And I'm just like everyone else. I was surprised to see that in the seven jobs I worked over fourteen months, I was complimented ten times. And yes, that worked. Each time I felt good about myself and my job.

I was shocked, though, at how few times managers used

recognition as a form of reward. I have studied rewards for more than 25 years. One of the things I look at is how people value the rewards I've covered in this chapter. From Dalian to Des Moines, and quite a few places in between, I've asked questions about rewards and their value to people in every socioeconomic group. Recognition, being told you did a good job, is universally highly regarded as a reward, regularly ranking in the top five in importance to employees. Although pay and job advancement opportunities regularly rank ahead of recognition as valued rewards, recognition has two advantages. Unlike pay, recognition is low cost. Praising an employee or having a pizza party to thank the team for beating an important production goal is a relatively inexpensive way of rewarding good performance.

Recognition also is special because it's one of the few rewards that supervisors actually control. If you think about it, supervisors have relatively little control over pay. The market determines most of what is given for starting pay, and the size of the budget for pay increases often determines the rest. Similarly, advancement opportunities aren't controlled by supervisors. A supervisor might make sure a favored employee has the skills to be promoted, but until an opening occurs, this reward can't be granted. And in a world where downsizing and flattening of organizations is a reality, this reward is becoming less prevalent. But recognition? Telling an employee "Good job"—that's a reward managers control and employees value. Despite this, most managers I worked with guarded praise as if it were a scarce commodity. When I asked one manager why she didn't have an Employee of the Month reward, she responded that she didn't want to disappoint the rest of her employees who didn't get the reward. My view was that if she had done it right, it would have given the rest of them something to aspire to.

Even though Kris was one of my best managers and did much to cultivate a positive and high-performing workplace, she was not as good as James at using praise as a reward. The only time I heard her tell anyone he or she had done well was on my last day at work. As I told her I had to leave, she asked me if I wanted to take a leave of absence, following this with a subtle compliment: "You fit in well with my people." These few words, tossed in almost as an afterthought, did much to make me feel good about this job.

One location I worked at actually had a formal recognition program. My first McDonald's gave crew members name tags that also had slots for little stick-on squares, much like those on military uniforms and used to acknowledge superior marksmanship or battle campaigns in hostile territories, and so on. Marie had four such markers, and she proudly noted they were for good work techniques and for knowledge about things like teamwork, fries, and safety. You could tell from Marie's face that these badges of valor were something special. Apparently the gold stars from our elementary school days still work even as we get older.

James had a gift for another form of reward—giving
feedback constructively. He had a natural knack for building feedback into conversations. While explaining to me that I was to learn sandwich assembly the next day, Michelle interrupted with an unsolicited observation that she didn't like that job. Almost seamlessly James launched into a discussion of Michelle's skillful handling of the takeout window but ended with an admonition that she needed to learn how to work assembly if she wanted to get ahead and that he had plans to help build her skills in this area. The same conversational tone for giving feedback and setting expectations also worked with me. He not only told me that I needed to speed up my placing of buns on the onion-covered burgers but also explained why. Not done correctly, the bun isn't infused with onion taste and smell—the signature of Krystal. James made constructive feedback and recognition a normal part of the work experience. And he saw giving these rewards as a part of his leadership responsibility in building and maintaining a good work environment.

Kris wasn't as good as James at giving recognition, but she was forceful and timely in giving feedback. One day Daniel, "the fast assembler," had more than his fill with Kyle, who despite 10 years of seniority still became flustered at lunch rush. Kyle's coping strategy was to ask others, usually new crew members, to do tasks that were rightfully his. On this day, Daniel finally took Kyle on, publicly telling him to do his job and stop expecting others to do it for him. From across the room, Kris immediately told Daniel, "ENOUGH." Just that one word. Later, she took him aside and explained to him that it was her job to correct employees and if he was unhappy, he should come to her for resolution. She closed by saying it would destroy morale if employees went around yelling at other crew members.

Many fast food workers view this employment as a first job, not as a career. If this is accurate, perhaps the most important reward a fast food job can provide is usable skills for life's later jobs. I would respond emphatically that this may be the major advantage of working in fast food. Important life skills are learned here! Indeed, I once talked to a high-level pharmaceutical executive whom I had told about my undercover work. His unsolicited rejoinder was resounding support for fast food jobs. He felt the discipline learned at an early age and the ability to cope with daily pressure were harbingers of future performance. I agree.

Training the Utterly Confused

ost experienced crew members I worked with saw training newbies as a necessary evil. To make matters worse, managers felt the same way. So what do you do when you have a task you don't like and don't necessarily find of value but are instructed by unenthusiastic managers to perform anyway? Your choices are don't do it and incur the kind of wrath that can kill a career quickly; do the job as quickly and as superficially as you can without incurring wrath; or delegate the job to someone else.

I worked with two managers who viewed training completely differently. First, they treated it not just as a way of building behaviors and developing skills in new employees but also as a way of building cultural awareness. They used training during the first days to say through deed and word: Here is what we stand for; here is what is important to us; and if you learn to fit into our culture, good things will happen. That's a lot to add onto the traditional skill indoctrination, but the good managers knew this. They tried to build relationships with rules: Learn the rules and what behaviors are important and our relationship—yours, mine, and the crew's—will flourish.

Why is an emphasis on the rules so important? Why do good fast food managers insist that training involves instilling behaviors much bigger than teaching how to put pickles

FROM BEHIND THE COUNTER

Managers' poor behavior is often echoed throughout the overall culture. The language of one employee, Freddy, is almost all profanity. And when other employees and, more importantly, customers can overhear Freddy's expletives, our manager Don angers quickly. In front of all of us, Don tells Freddy if he can't clean up his language, he will "pull his hours." I interpret this to mean he will be fired. Don further rides Freddy on every mistake he makes, and he laces most of the feedback with sarcasm. Although Freddy is much better at his job than are some of the other crew members, he is also more trouble, and Don wants to minimize trouble first. Hence, why I was hired. Don wants to try to change the culture. And this means changing more than behaviors for processing orders; it also involves all the behaviors that are needed in other tasks and interactions. He has too many kids who stand around and talk about the latest party—never is the customer first. I guess he figures us old geezers will be more customer-focused, and all for $6.25 an hour (I made $16.75 my first day).

on a burger correctly? To answer this, you need to go back to a time when you did something completely foreign to you. For most new crew members, that's what a fast food job is. For some, it's their first time working. For others it may not be a first job, but it's definitely different from any job they have ever had. The only analogous situation I can re-member in my life was the first few days of college, which was my first time without Mom and Dad. Whatever the cir-cumstance, for many people, "new" equals "scary," and they'd rather face new with someone else whose bravado—false or not—provides the strength they need. This is what a new fast food job feels like to most of the newly hired crew mem-bers. I too felt the stress of being new at that first job at Arby's. So building relationships, even with those with whom you wouldn't normally bond, is essential. And good man-agers work at cultivating a tight-knit crew. On my first job, I found myself befriending a 20-year-old whose claim to fame was a vocabulary composed almost entirely of four-letter words. And as if that wasn't a big enough leap into the un-known, I also tried to bond with a heavy-metal rocker.

While Don understood the importance of culture, his training methods focused solely on behaviors needed to process orders. When I or others made mistakes, he un-leashed sarcastic salvos. I didn't like him, and I took the first opportunity to connect with someone—anyone—for com-miseration. For the first few days, until Freddy and Randy (a heavy-metal freak) began to wear thin, I tried to under-stand and befriend them. While I didn't adopt their behav-iors, I also didn't adopt Don's, and he lost a chance to mold me into what he had hoped for—the first representative of a new culture.

Good managers take training as an opportunity to build a relationship with new hires who are highly impressionable during those first few days. We want nothing more than to

FROM BEHIND THE COUNTER

Telling me what behaviors are important and why goes a long way toward making every job an important one. Introducing me to the rest of the crew and pointing out what they do well and what needs to be changed goes far in creating a performance-driven culture. While getting me an ID number, James shows me the overhead cameras and names each employee. Later, at Nicky's urging, James does in-person introductions. For my first hour of work, James basically stays with me. He tells me exactly what I will do: Start on cooking and move to sandwich assembly when things are a bit slower. As he shows me the grill area, James explains how to load the meat, onions, and rolls. He notes the buzzer going off, and he tells me that when I'm proficient, I should be able to load a whole grill with burgers before that first buzzer goes off. Then he explains that a second buzzer signals the deadline for applying the dehydrated onions to each of the approximately 64 burgers on each grill. I've got about two minutes after that to place buns on top of each burger and close the grill hood over the cooking meat. James actually tells me why, which is something no one else has ever explained. I feel like I matter to James. Krystal's secret to success is a bun and meat infused with the smell of onions. Who knew?

Tomorrow comes all too quickly. My back aches from cooking over a grill that is too low for my height, but I'm eager to meet James's challenge. Before I can even begin, James stops me and tells me what good work I did yesterday. Other crew members support his welcome words, and I am surprisingly touched by this simple gesture of recognition.

understand the rules and to make it through the first day without being embarrassed. We look forward to a time when we too can claim, with bravado, "Aw, this job is easy." Good managers take advantage of this opportunity and mind-set.

James actually wasn't the best trainer I worked with; others did a better job of explaining some of the tasks I had to perform. But he was one of the best managers, especially in teaching me how to be a good employee. By spending unusual amounts of time with me the first day, when I was so nervous (despite being an old pro who had started numerous other jobs in recent months), he built a quick attachment and sowed the seeds of a strong relationship. I was grateful to him for easing those first days of work. And because he told me what behaviors he expected and when, I clearly knew what it took to keep him happy. More than anyone else I had worked with, I wanted James to be pleased with my performance. Here I was, twice this manager's age, and yet I was curiously grateful for his attention. No other manager did such a good job of linking the social side of the job to the training task with such clear behavior rules and expectations.

I've made several hundred speeches in my life—one of them before 4,000 people—and you'd think that would be sufficient terror for one lifetime. None of these experiences, though, prepared me for the terror of working the front counter without enough (or sometimes any) training. At both Arby's and my second McDonald's, I was put on the front counter from the very start. Before I even knew what was on the menu, I was taking orders. Arby's at least attempted some prior training, but McDonald's did not. Picture this nightmare: One minute I had someone looking over my shoulder, telling me what to do, making me think maybe with this kind of help I might get through the day. But when I turned to ask a question, the trainer was gone! It was lunch rush, and he had his own job to do. My first reaction was panic. The lines were getting longer. There was no sign on the front marquee saying, "Don't eat here. Trainee is slow and stupid."

Unsuspecting customers came through the door and chose my line, expecting reasonably fast delivery. The sight of that line made cold sweat run down the brim of my recycled hat. Generally, people didn't yell at me when I made mistakes, but I could see the looks of disdain in their eyes as they mentally asked themselves how they ended up with me. My internal monitor screamed at me, "Don't do this! Flee! Flee now!" No doubt many other first timers have experienced this, and often enough, that inner voice won. People quit—lots of them—in their first few days. Usually they quit because the training was so poor that they wondered if they would ever get the hang of it or if the feeling of intense pressure would ever subside. In general, I found training to be inadequate. The best training I got was from Arby's (the above scene notwithstanding) and Wendy's; the worst was from the two McDonald's.

Neither Arby's nor Krystal had DVD training. Everything was taught and learned on the job. When I worked at the Big Three (McDonald's, Burger King, and Wendy's), I generally spent part of the first day watching DVDs. I was more impressed with the production quality than with the training content. McDonald's had a general orientation DVD. They tried to convince me the job would be chock full of rewards: Friends! New skills! Advancement! Providing a valued service!!! I was making $5.50 an hour, so they had already lost me at "Friends!" Both Burger Kings, conversely, focused almost entirely on building skills. There were different DVDs for many of the major jobs (such as the broiler and sandwich assembly) and for several general issues (sanitation and safety). At different points in the sessions, the DVDs would stop and give me a pop quiz. Some of the questions were silly: I didn't know where Burger King headquarters was (Miami), so they made me watch that part of the DVD again. I sure didn't know how many employees Burger King had (350,000): Watch the DVD again, Jerry. In fairness, many of their questions were good. They wanted us to wash our hands for 20 seconds. The subsequent quiz asked me to guesstimate what constituted 20 seconds. Wrong again; watch again.

Wendy's video was hilarious, but I don't think intentionally. In one scene a guy was shown neglecting to wash his hands. A kind of blue haze settled over him, and then the haze transferred to everything he touched. In the last scene as "haze man" walked up the front steps of a suburban tract house, his son rushed out to hug him, and the haze enveloped them both. Cut to fade. It was like *Leave It to Beaver* meets *The Blob*. Despite these occasional laughs, I found watching three hours of tapes incredibly boring. Presentations were repetitive and slow to develop. I was reluctant to get up and stretch or go to the bathroom because the Burger King manager had informed me she had her eye on another girl hired just before me who had left to go to the bathroom three times.

What's wrong with the DVD experience? A few things. DVDs are a fine way to present general information, but they need to be as realistic as possible. Not once did a DVD presentation convey how insane every fast food job was during lunch rush. When Karen showed viewers how to make a sandwich on the DVD, she explained each step slowly, the whole process taking about three minutes. Karen was cool and her hair was perfect. She didn't have a drop of sweat or even a hand-me-down hat, and there wasn't a sound except her calm, quiet voice explaining what she was doing. Well, that's not how it was in the real world. Let's look at some *real* assembly experiences.

My first McDonald's assembly experience was not the success story portrayed by DVD Karen. I was assembling sandwiches—a job one crew member told me was the easiest job in the place—and before I knew it, my back started aching, the afternoon rush became more pressured and chaotic, and I found myself swimming in sandwiches! The pace was relentless: Which one gets dehydrated onion? Which gets real onion? How many pickles? How many pieces of cheese? There are three kinds of sauce dispensed out of caulking tubes. Which sauce is in which tube, and which goes on which sandwich? Does everything get ketchup and mustard? There are at least four kinds of rolls, one of which gets toasted. Which one? I was hopelessly lost!

Exposing trainees to a working environment that is dramatically different from what's represented on the DVD negates anything useful they could have possibly taken from the training experience. The behaviors I learned in training didn't fit the reality I faced every day. If I had to guess, I would say that things weren't done the training manual way at least 25 percent of the time. Every DVD preached about discarding old product: Buns shouldn't be left in warmer trays more than 30 minutes; fries should be discarded if they've sat for more than 7 minutes; you get the picture. At Wendy's, I took my training to heart, but every time I tried to discard product, I was told to just push the timer button again and let the fries sit. Crew members and managers alike violated DVD rules. For instance, we were supposed to take hot potatoes out of the oven with mitts, but my manager grabbed two with bare hands, making sure to caution me not to do this myself. Was this a "Don't try this at home" moment? The reality of fast food impinged on the DVD version so often that it was almost comical. It became difficult to decide which behaviors were important and which were to be ignored. The mixed message and ambiguity caused tension and sometimes planted the seed for fleeing—unnecessary turnover.

At Burger King, I had a hard time figuring out the rules. They changed depending on whom you talked to and who was watching. Some rules were enforced only when a manager was looking. Every paper wrapper for sandwiches at Burger King had to be marked during sandwich assembly with a discard time (note: this requirement has since been eliminated). Any sandwich still unsold after that time was to be thrown out, and managers took these times very seriously. Crew members, in contrast, simply understood that the rule was moot. It took little time to reason that burgers made to order never sat around (every store I worked at made burgers to order—during the lunch shift nothing ever got wrapped that wasn't already ordered). Why waste three seconds per order marking this useless piece of information? Some behaviors were enforced more strictly when you were new. Not to worry: Sanitation rules were always enforced; these were taken quite seriously. But the level of expected compliance dropped from absurd to reasonable after the first few training days. I found that as the new guy, I was watched more carefully and corrected for doing things routinely done by more senior crew members. I finally had enough when Taylor came over and noticed that I had pushed the paper towel lever while my hands were still soaped up. I had planned to do the full 20-second drill, but I had forgotten the towels. If I touched the towel dispenser after washing, I had contaminated my hands and I needed to start over. Taylor ran through the full routine. I waited semipatiently as he demonstrated drying his hands, and just as he went to shut off the water, I pointed out that he had just touched the two faucets, which were no doubt teeming with germs. I should have been fired for being a wise guy, but the double standard finally got to me. To his credit, Taylor admitted the practice had flaws, but he wanted me to understand the way it was supposed to be done.

Some rules were selectively enforced depending on how busy the store was, and others were completely disregarded. This treatment of the rules and codes was certainly not taught during the DVD training sessions. And paying selective attention to the rules is not exclusive to fast food. Many organizations find that processes are abandoned during the heat of business, and they consequently struggle with making the training of their managers and employees relevant.

Wendy's provided a good lesson in making training as effective as possible. The company's formal program included both DVDs and pamphlets. Watch the DVD at the store, take home the supporting pamphlet for nighttime reading. (I took them home; others read them on-site.) However, the reason Wendy's did training right is that the company had identified which behaviors taught to new employees were critical to their business. So much so that the behaviors were linked to the company's incentive system: Managers got incentives for the training performance of new crew members. When we demonstrated that we knew the desired behaviors, managers were rewarded. Unfortunately, I came about this information the hard way.

FROM BEHIND THE COUNTER

After I finished reading the pamphlet, Cindy asked if I had answered the questions included throughout. I thought she was joking—first because they were labeled as "discussion questions," not "exam questions," and second because she seemed so serious. Half in jest, I asked if I would be graded. My big mouth got me a glare and a sharp "Yes!" Later that day I discovered Orville marking my answers in the manager's office. I'm pretty sure I got at least one wrong. They asked me the four reasons we sanitize: I knew three. My fourth guess was, "So the customers don't die, allowing them to come back and eat more Triple Burgers." If I'd known how seriously they took this, maybe I wouldn't have been such a wise guy.

While DVD training had its drawbacks, on-the-job instruction was a recipe for hypertension. Every store assigned someone, maybe multiple someones, to shadow new employees, teaching them how to perform tasks. Often those chosen to train reflected that employee's promise. Only good employees were designated trainers, which made sense. But this didn't necessarily make them good trainers or managers. Once I did have someone who was good at training, but more often, I ran into the same three training mistakes:

1. When business heated up, trainers went to other jobs.

2. We "practiced" on real products and had little opportunity to learn when no customers were waiting. This added tension and, I'm convinced, slowed the learning process.

3. We received contradictory instructions—or no instructions at all.

It stands to reason that when the pressure mounts, new hires need a shadow more than ever. But too often I found that to be just the time the shadow crew member disappeared. Managers in fast food, like those everywhere, are often asked to do more—and more and more—with less. Which is why, when dollars count, it is ineffective for the business to have new employees practice with real product where every damaged order represents lost revenue and investment. Because the order screen dictated what the subsequent orders were, I seldom got a chance to practice what the trainer had just shown me. By the time another Grilled Chicken came up, I couldn't remember the prior instruction. Because I had never practiced the same sandwich twice in a row, it took me a long time to see the pattern. When I went home at night from my first McDonald's job, I actually constructed a grid with sandwiches listed down the side and possible ingredients along the top. Each sandwich got a check mark in the appropriate cells. The next day I asked Luis, the shift supervisor, if my grid was right. He made a couple of corrections, and he kept a copy since the store had no visual training aid.

FROM BEHIND THE COUNTER

Ron takes me outside to show me how to police the area. Ron is a 70-something Georgia Good Ole Boy who is missing four teeth in the lower front. He's a nice guy who works hard, but he insists on showing me how to sweep up cigarette butts with a broom and dustpan. After I've "got it," he continues to follow me around, pointing out trash. Apparently everyone thinks I'm an idiot.

I gave Arby's good marks because of their training technology. All of their POS registers had a training mode. Enter a code and you could practice to your heart's content without the "annoyance and terror" of actual customers. Even with this training aid, though, my first real experience with customers was traumatic. Word often got around that I was a little slower than the others to pick up on things. The result, as this Wendy's behind-the-counter story illustrates, was sometimes comedic.

Many times, I either got contradictory instructions or got none at all. Use the tongs to feed patties into the broiler. Don't use tongs; it's too slow. At McDonald's, I was told to keep two Small Fries in holding slot A, four Medium in B, two Large in C, and no Super (on demand only) in D. Sara, the store manager, gave me these directions, but they were different from those I got from Julie, another worker, who had said to keep a Super in a holding tray too. Sara demanded

FROM BEHIND THE COUNTER

So whose instructions to follow became a constant worry, as did maintaining a positive relationship with managers whose rules I may have questioned in the past.

Applying the principle that initiative is a good thing, I go to the back storage area, find a sponge, load it with some disinfectant and soap, get some paper towels, and proceed to wipe down my fry area. Sara sees me and is clearly miffed, but I'm not sure why. Have I disobeyed an order? I have nothing to do, and I want to act busy by cleaning up. All the other staff with charge areas are cleaning their stations. Seeing me, and apparently judging that I'm doing it wrong, Sara tells me she doesn't have time to train me and that I can go home early. I interpret this as a reprimand. For what, I'm not sure. Later that night as I play things over in my mind, I link this incident to an earlier one:

I'm working fry station, and at one point Sara hands me a packing/storage box and says to get more of these. It's unclear what she wants, so I read the box label to try and figure it out. Two days ago, I would have just asked, but questions seem to be treated with hostility, so I'm reluctant. The first line on the box is gibberish mixed with the words "Dog Happy Meal" (packaging labels are the earliest known form of hieroglyphics—the Rosetta Stone actually begins with the letters U, P, and S). I deduce she needs more of the toys. I get them, go out front, and am about to dump them where the other toys are, but it's almost full. What gives? I point this out, and in an exasperated tone, Sara says, "No, I want boxes!" I can't figure out what she means—does she mean empty boxes? Finally, she says she needs Happy Meal boxes. It's the first time she has uttered these words. I grant, in looking back, I could have been a lot smarter, but the pressure is to move quickly, not to think. I get the boxes; she takes some out for immediate use and leaves me with the remainder. Because she's so busy, I'm hesitant to ask where the remainder go, and I'm reluctant to go exploring because the activity level up front is fever-ish, and my station, which I have left to hunt down boxes, sorely needs me. Because the Happy Meal boxes seem central to Sara's needs at the time, I leave them up front temporarily but out of the walkway. I rush back to my fries, which are quickly depleting. A minute later Sara angrily says, "Jerry, put the boxes there!" The word "there" is illustrated by a sweeping hand gesture that could mean any of several places. Since there are no signs in any of the possible stor-age areas, and no logical way to deduce which is correct, I ask her where, and as she angrily points to a more specific location, I'm pretty sure I have sealed my fate with her.

In retrospect, I'm sure this exchange precipitated her later decision to tell me to go home. Shortened hours are one form of punishment—a first warning. I wonder how I could have gone from darling one day to goat the next.

to know who had told me this. Thinking quickly about all the old movies I had seen with the stoolie getting knifed by another inmate, I decided to tell her I wasn't going to say. I think this angered her. Later, when I had a free minute, I decided to clean my fry workstation, and I asked Sara about the proper procedure. Exasperated, she told me, "With towels!"

But what does a good training program look like?

On one side are the folks—some of my colleagues and most of the fast food industry, I suspect—who say that cheap and fast is best. Throw us into the job, assign someone to coach as time permits, and let Darwin prevail. The strong shall survive; the weak will quit. What's wrong with that?

An argument can be made that high turnover is economically defensible. I worked four jobs that bought into this philosophy of training. I'm rating these stores purely from an employee's perspective. Were early anxieties minimized, and how thorough was the skills training? Two stores did pretty well overall: They tried to prepare me by building skills before throwing me to the burger wolves. To my first Burger King and only Wendy's, I say "Thanks!" If I were giving out letter grades, Wendy's would get an A– and the Burger King in New York would get a B+. Krystal and my first McDonald's would come in a close third and get B grades. Arby's would have earned an A, certainly, for their training technology, but everything else was abysmal—a C grade. My second Burger King and McDonald's lagged way behind—a D grade.

The best training always had the same ingredients. Managers isolated important behaviors, found a way to convey that they were important (remember Kris; she assigned someone who had mastered specific tasks to be a special mentor), and kept close watch to make sure that these behaviors were being learned and demonstrated accurately. Both Kris at Burger King and James at Krystal made big-time investments in my training from our very first meeting on. I'm convinced this reaped huge time savings later on.

Diversity, Discrimination, and Lap Dancing

I once did some consulting work for a sports apparel manufacturer. The company owner had discovered a ready and reliable supply of Vietnamese workers. All went well for a while. Soon, however, the Vietnamese workers reached a critical mass and became a substantial and increasingly vocal minority. Then the clashes began. "Us versus them" replaced "We." English-speaking workers complained about everything being conducted in two languages, including training sessions. Then job security threats began to pop up. The Vietnamese were working together better and garnering bigger team incentives. Verbal clashes became physical. The solution in this case was to move the Vietnamese to a separate plant, which was coincidentally needed because of rapid expansion. A similar problem arose in my fast food experiences.

Every store I worked in had significant numbers of employees from minority groups. Most times I saw no evidence of problems, but there were two exceptions: the first in a Wendy's near Jacksonville, Florida, and the second in a McDonald's in the heartland of Michigan. The Wendy's crew was split about evenly between blacks and whites. The Mc-

Donald's had nearly as many Hispanics as non-Hispanics. In both these stores I felt a noticeable clash of cultures that was exacerbated, I think, by the segregation of jobs. Wendy's had most of the blacks working the counter and drive-thru jobs and the whites working the assembly jobs. The exact opposite segregating took place at McDonald's: All of the assembly jobs were filled by Hispanics and other minorities, and the customer contact jobs were filled by non-Hispanics. Both stores had, I think, unhealthy group dynamics. Management should not have ignored these problems. The crews' jobs were difficult enough without adding the negatives of crew-versus-crew friction.

Unprovoked clashes punctuated my Michigan McDonald's experience. In most of the stores I'd worked in, customer wishes drove the work process. If a customer changed his or her mind and wanted no mustard, that was no problem unless the order already had been submitted. The counter person didn't have a mechanism to quickly change an order that was already on the screen in the back assembly area, so protocol dictated that the counter person called back a verbal change to the assembler. The assembler acknowledged hearing the counter person, and all was well that ended well. Not in this MickeyD's though. These assemblers seemed to have selective language skills. Use the right tone of voice, make the change sound like a request, and the change was quickly processed. But in the heat of lunch rush, forget yourself and simply yell out a change, and nothing happened. In most places, counter trumps assembler.

Getting a customer's change right and fast meant abandoning niceties. At this McDonald's, though, culture trumped customer. Don't show the proper deference and the language problem arose. José, the only bilingual crew member in the store, must be hunted down and the change translated through him into Spanish. Maybe this civility should be the norm in all stores, but the reality of lunch rush pressure usually means commands are flung fast, it's not personal, and what happens during rush stays in rush. Not here, though.

I'm convinced that subgroups inherently reach a critical mass. Below this number, working with people from widely diverse backgrounds and accommodating those cultural differences are physical and emotional necessities. But above the critical mass, intra-group bonding allows most needs to be met within the group so there's no longer a need to venture out into the different, unfamiliar customs of those outside one's central group. Diversity is good, but when two different groups approach equal size, too often struggles for supremacy begin. Lesson to be learned? Most of the research on diversity recommends exploring the full panorama of differences among people.[1] Narrow the number of differences,

---

1 D. Pollitt, "Diversity is about more than observing the letter of the law," *Human Resource Management International Digest*, vol. 13, no. 4, 2005, pp. 37–40.

and no matter how economically pragmatic, trouble may follow.

Do fast food restaurants discriminate? The answer is an emphatic "NO!" I saw people of every nationality in my seven jobs. Stores are populated by males and females, older workers and younger workers. The promotion pipeline also was clogged with the right mix of people. Over the years I've consulted with hundreds of companies, and none of them could boast a better mix of genders, ages, and nationalities than I saw across these seven stores. While fast food restaurants may not discriminate, they do seem to be influenced by traditional views of what work goes to whom. Here are a few of the ways jobs are allotted by gender, age, and sometimes nationality.

Although I saw guys who worked the front counter (including me) or the drive-thru window, most times these jobs seemed to be held by women. This practice fit the stereotype that women are gentler and more sociable—all the better to appear less threatening and to carry on brief conversations with customers. Women also disproportionately held the top jobs in my stores: Only in my first and last jobs were men the store managers. Interestingly, the shift managers and assistant managers were a healthy mix of males and females.

Guys got the maintenance and general stocking jobs. When trucks needed to be unloaded, it was always a guy assigned to the job. Seasoned workers liked to delegate the physical jobs to new male crew members. My worst experience happened in my first McDonald's. This store was built on two levels, so it was a major hassle to carry food products from the refrigerator and freezer in the basement up to the cooking areas on the first floor. I spent too much of my second day hauling cases of burgers and fries up the stairs. With my bad hip and back, this was an agonizing challenge. And like many seniors, I was too proud to admit that this job was more than I could handle. I still picture myself as the 20-year-old summer construction worker, spending all day carrying blocks and mixing "mud" for demanding brick masons. Struggling to lift 40-pound boxes up 18 cellar steps just wasn't who I wanted to admit I'd become.

Every store had a contingent of older workers. They never held the sandwich assembly jobs. Those jobs required good eyesight for reading the hieroglyphics on the computer screen and fast motor skills for making sandwiches quickly. I guess it was assumed that our eyes weren't good enough and our motors weren't fast enough. So the seniors tended to get periphery jobs. Sometimes this meant doing prep work like making salads or soups. Other times it meant being assigned to the front register (again usually the women) or the front lobby. This latter job was one part host, one part cleanup.

Workers who spoke halting English never had jobs with exposure to customers. Remember the store in Michigan where half the crew spoke Spanish? As best I could determine, they had learned just enough English to do their jobs. The maintenance guy fixed things using the "point-and-repair method"—you pointed at something that didn't work and he repaired it. The sandwich assembly crew, all Latino, understood when you said, "No mustard," but when you attempted to talk about most other things, they would stare back quizzically. Ever pragmatic, though, fast food stores loved these employees because they could make sandwiches fast and they showed up every day. The key to equality is the ability to perform; fast food is all about performance. And reliability.

※　　※　　※

The fast food industry strives for diversity in its work-

force. Recruitment brochures and ads for fast food all have the requisite mix of colors, nationalities, ages, and genders. As I've stated, fast food stores don't practice discrimination. But they do not practice "inclusion" either. Embracing diversity is about recognizing, accommodating, and even gaining from individual differences. For example, I don't learn very well when I'm told something—I have to see it to learn it. Others learn better from hearing than seeing. Accommodating both learning styles is accepting and encouraging workforce diversity, or at least the scratched surface of diversity. But *diversity* defined this way, the kind that goes below the cosmetic differences of skin color or native language, is very hard, if not impossible, for fast food chains to accommodate. In the quest for speed and efficiency, fast food stores design everything for their image of their "average" worker. I hadn't even started my first job when I became embarrassingly aware of how routine fast food procedures are. Not only are the fast food rules "one size fits all," but so are the physical work layouts. The width of aisles in work areas is sufficient for two average workers to walk unimpeded, or for one to walk past another working at a station, with neither worrying about bumping the other. Put a few extra pounds on one or both of these frames, though, and the impeding begins.

While all these insensitivities to different body structures bothered me, indeed hurt me physically, I shouldn't hold the fast food industry to a higher standard than the rest of the world. Very few mainstream products or workstations are designed to accommodate any but minor deviations from "average."

Where I do blame fast food, though, is on the plus side of diversity. Embracing diversity in the workforce requires accommodating not only differences in physical attributes but also differences in viewpoints. Properly nurtured, these different ways of looking at the world can yield insights about better ways to work. I half expected that my opinions wouldn't matter much in fast food jobs—after all, I was new and inexperienced. I wasn't prepared, though, to have my every suggestion, no matter how logically made, ignored.

I knew when I started this project my biggest challenge would be to resist exercising the hinges in my jaw. I'm in a profession where talking isn't only encouraged, it's mandated. The very words "lecturing to students" mean that I talk, and it feeds my soul (or perhaps my craving for attention) to know that my every word is valued, if only because the next exam might depend on remembering it. That background is not good training for fast foods, where there is only one way

FROM BEHIND THE COUNTER

Thomas is the owner's son, and he regularly comes in at lunch rush to help out. He clearly doesn't have to, and because of this I have a positive impression of him. Others also seem to like him. When he says he can handle this whole lunch rush by himself, several hoot at him and jokingly offer to leave and let him try. He seems approachable, and I make the mistake of doing just this. I've noticed for the past several days that Burger King makes chili meat by cooking pristine new burgers, crumbling them up, and adding them as the meat component. Meanwhile I've been instructed to throw away any burgers that tear during the cooking process. Why, I reason, shouldn't we use these burgers in the chili, saving several dollars a day? It all adds up, doesn't it? I introduce myself to Thomas and tell him my idea, but as I'm talking, I can see his eyes diverting to other things. He isn't listening, and he has probably already dismissed my idea. Before I finish, he interrupts and tells me my idea would constitute a health code violation and that we can't do it. Before I can say anything, he walks away. I've been dismissed. I'm steamed, so I'm glad he has left. I'm sure I would have blurted out that the Wendy's I worked at just down the street uses the very procedure I recommended here.

to do every job. Even though I had read about this in books, I didn't believe it: Surely most workers were recognized by their employers as being able to provide valid insight on more efficient ways of working, gained from hundreds, even thousands, of repetitions. But my assumption proved wrong. Employees do indeed make improvements on the way management tells them to get their jobs done. Behind management's back, I heard employees in every store suggest to other employees some nonstandard ways of doing their jobs. The bun doesn't go through the toaster rack quickly enough? Squish it down with your hand slightly. Taking the buns out of the warmer bins is awkward? Place them in the bin in the opposite direction; they're easier to pull out. The way nearly every job was supposed to be done was improved by a smart worker intent on making things easier. But those improvements never seemed to work their way up the management chain.

I'm convinced that fast food managers don't think most fast food workers are very intelligent. This appears to be their assumption going in. The professed goal of fast food is to make every job simple enough that the next operation naturally follows from the last. Don't think, just react. And if you think, keep it to yourself. So many tasks in fast food are routine that little comes up for which a standard procedure doesn't exist. This takes thinking out of the job, and because workers don't have to think most times, managers come to believe that they can't think. This is my theory, and I'm sticking with it! Certainly every time I tried to make suggestions, violating my rule about trying to keep my mouth shut, I was greeted with silence—the most positive response—or, worse, condescension.

Maintaining a healthy work environment goes beyond

accommodating gender, age, and nationality. An individual's personal behavior can likewise create a hostile workplace. In this section, I'll tell you two stories: the Lap Dancer and Lolita.

Many of the training DVDs I watched warned against sexual harassment, something prohibited under the Civil Rights Act. Don, the manager at Arby's, gave a fairly typical warning when he said, "This is important upstairs, so don't do it!" Two types of behavior are prohibited. The first is obvious: Don't seek sexual favors in exchange for giving a better job situation (for example, a raise, promotion, or even favorable work hours). I saw no signs of this kind of behavior. The second type of harassment is much less concrete. If you do something—most frequently packaged with a sexual wrapping—and it causes another employee discomfort, you may be guilty of creating a hostile work environment. There are a lot of gray areas within this definition, so, to be on the safe side, the DVDs simply warned, "Don't do anything that might make someone uncomfortable." No sexual jokes, no suggestive pictures, and no flirtatious behaviors or even friendly touching. The list of no's is both lengthy and ambiguous. Some behaviors, though, are unmistakably wrong. I think lap dancing falls squarely into that category.

FROM BEHIND THE COUNTER

It's my second day at one of the stores (name withheld for obvious reasons). So far I like Ann, but I don't know what to think when I see her "act."

I manage to get through a lunch rush without causing anyone else delays. When things slow down, the crew collectively breathes easier. As I finish cleaning my work area, I hear the sounds of joyous laughter. It's not like fast food people to visibly celebrate, yet there is clearly fun being had somewhere. Then I notice a crowd of crew members has gathered to watch Ann, the store manager, in her office bouncing on the lap of a crew member who I later learned was Jay, one of the top sandwich assemblers. No one seems surprised, but this behavior is so out of place that I'm stunned. I glance at the few crew members not congregated in front of the manager's door, and it's business as usual.

About two weeks after I quit this particular job, I decided to violate my initial protocol—I planned on warning Ann, the store manager, of the dangers looming because of her behavior. I entered the restaurant around 3 p.m., long enough after lunch rush that I would be able to talk with her privately. Once she was seated, I reminded her that I'm a professor, and, for the first time, I explained that I teach human resources management, including sexual harassment

Ten days later it happens again! For all the crew to see, Ann is bouncing up and down on the lap of Jeff, the assistant manager. I'm no longer stunned, but the professor in me is trying to decide what to do. I can't warn Ann; I've pledged I will do my job and only my job while I'm an employee, but later that day I find a way to keep my oath and still caution Ann. As I am working the second assembly board, Larry at first board is telling a very off-color joke. In any other setting I would consider this action as harassment, but compared to Ann's lap dancing, it seems almost docile. When he finishes, I stage whisper in what I hope will be taken as a joking voice, "Sexual harassment, sexual harassment." Before anyone else reacts, Ann, who overhears both the joke and my comment, exclaims, "It's only harassment if they don't like it!" She's wrong—if only one crew member feels uneasy about any of these antics, we have a classic case of hostile work environment harassment.

issues. I led by explaining that only two days earlier a sexual harassment class-action suit had been filed against a major fast food franchiser. Then I recounted her earlier "performance." (See the above "From Behind the Counter.") She retorted with "It's not harassment if they like it." I explained to her why she was wrong: "Think about Arthur." I asked her to think about the 11-year veteran who has climbed only one rung on the advancement ladder in all this time. "He sees you 'favoring' two employees, both of whom have less seniority and are moving up faster than he is. I think a judge would rule in favor of Arthur, should he pursue it." As I was finishing, my message began to sink in. Ann's face was getting increasingly paler. As I left, I hoped I had convinced her about the inappropriateness of her behavior.

Sexual harassment isn't just a boss-employee problem. In fact, in fast food I suspect employee-employee incidents are much more likely. Throw together a workforce in which two-thirds of the employees are under 20 years of age,[2] mix the genders, and watch hormones activate. Budding romances were a regular theme at all my jobs. I had ready access to these ongoing soap operas. Because I was the age of most of these kids' parents, I was marginalized just as their parents were: It was as if I wasn't there. Only once did I have any extended conversations with someone under the drinking age. Forgive me if I call her "Lolita," but it's for a good reason. Of all the young crew members I met, Lolita was the only one who acted as if the difference in our ages wasn't an inviolable barrier. From the first day, Lolita smiled, engaged, and eventually even touched me. To be fair, she was a "toucher," sometimes even hugging people when she was particularly happy. Sometimes she went too far, though, making sexually charged comments even to me, which made me feel both confused and uncomfortable.

---

2 Eric Schlosser, *Fast Food Nation: The Dark Side of the All-American Meal* (Boston: Houghton Mifflin, 2001).

I understand now why sexual harassment was such a prominent theme in my orientation training. These kids were working during a substantial part of their available free time. That meant that their job became, for many, their social outlet. In some ways this socializing was good for the stores, and it was encouraged: Come to work—it's where your friends are. However, every action causes a reaction, and these establishments need to be extra careful that these relationships are conducted within the constraints established by the sexual harassment laws. In addition, good managers need to model consistently appropriate behavior that encourages camaraderie but stays within professional boundaries.

I Blame It on Henry Ford

Supersized Management Principle

Build social webs and cultivate
camaraderie in order to reduce turnover
in volatile industries.

worked in one store with just over 100 percent turnover (low for the industry) and another in the same chain with 500 percent turnover. Why the difference? There were disparities in the way they hired people: One was extremely diligent in interviewing and selecting candidates; the other spent as little time as possible. Both paid identical wages and used pretty much the same DVDs to train employees. But I'm convinced the major difference was in store leadership.

In the low-turnover store the manager worked hard to create friendships among the crew members. Key to this store manager's success was a crew member named Daniel. He had a whole host of interests, and he loved finding people who shared them. One was computer games, an addiction he shared with several other crew members. I overheard one conversation he had with Larry, the regular drive-thru guy. Each bragged about his prowess, all centered on who got to what level of what game. Part of Daniel's appeal, though, was generosity. Daniel's insider knowledge of these games, gained through countless all-nighters (a fact punctuated by the bags under his tired 23-year-old eyes), was willingly shared with anyone interested in listening. Daniel also was a Hacky Sack junkie. Between challenges to others, he would answer questions about the fine art of juggling and passing. If no one was interested, the Hacky Sack became a playful weapon, tossed at some unsuspecting crew member when the manager wasn't looking and used to stir up a game of one-upmanship.

Perhaps Daniel's biggest gift, though, was his ability to be interested in—and create interest among—people who seemed not to have any commonalities. Take me, for example: I was more than twice his age; my last serious computer game was Pong, invented before Daniel was born; and I couldn't balance a Hacky Sack on my foot even if it were superglued on. But I still liked Daniel. He found out I was a semiretired professor. As a college graduate, he made sure we had something in common. He asked me if any of my students were like him; what he needed to do to get into graduate school; and whether I thought it would get him out of this job (which he admitted later was an "okay" job). I found myself interested in Daniel, as were the others. The store manager, Kris, recognized this and made sure Daniel got plenty of hours. When the lunch shift crew was there, Daniel was there. And so on. Kris was building what I've come to call a "social web." Her goal was to "stick" crew members to the web, making it harder to leave. The glue of this web was friendship, and at the center of this web of friendship was Daniel.

I've come to discover since working at this Burger King that social relations are a powerful force for keeping crew members tied to a job and store. When you work 20 to 40 hours a week at a wage just peeking above minimum, you need some reason to go to work every day. Money wasn't the reason—there are lots of low-paying jobs in this world. Kris discovered on her own that friendship was a very good reason. I remember one manager who hadn't discovered this important lesson. Orville at Wendy's discouraged making his store the social hub for his workers. One former worker, though having long since migrated to another fast food store, often visited Wendy's because, as he told me while waiting for break times, he still had good friends working there.

Now contrast Kris's crew with the store with 500 percent turnover. No crew member wore a name tag. Neither the manager nor the assistant managers introduced me to anyone, including the people who were to train me. Oh, sure, I was told Emily would train me, but this was more a transmission of information than an introduction. At one point on the second day, not having been introduced yet to the manager (I was hired by a second-shift supervisor), I mistook an assistant manager for Angela, the top person. "I'm not Angela," she said indignantly, pointing to the front of the store and waving in a general direction. "That's her up there." The store was partitioned such that, from the assembly area, I couldn't see the face of someone standing at the counter. All I could see was someone's back, which meant that I still couldn't tell who Angela was.

The only way I met anyone in this store was by introducing myself, something I did out of frustration several days later. (You'll recall my "experiment" from Chapter 3.) Even after meeting several others, though, I wasn't enthusiastic about building these relationships. One crew member was Angela's sister, Tina, the poster child for why nepotism is a bad idea. Tina had mountains of attitude that, fortunately, wasn't wasted on a newbie like me. She socialized only with

Ellen, who, it turned out, was Angela's best friend. All three of them drove together to work, and this (un)holy trinity created the exact opposite of a social web. No one hung around at this store to talk with others when a shift was over. I was glad to get out of there. If this store hadn't been a rich source of information about how *not* to run a store, I suspect I wouldn't have lasted even a week. Then again, at 500 percent turnover, staying only a week was not especially unusual.

Most statistics I have seen show that turnover hovers

around 200 to 250 percent for crew members in fast food restaurants. This means that if you open a new store on January 1, by the middle of the year everyone has quit. You start over again, and by the end of the year everyone has quit again. Decade after decade you have to repopulate the store twice per year. It's no wonder that Rich Floersch, corporate head of human resources at McDonald's, is proud of the way the company has reduced turnover to somewhere between 100 and 150 percent. And the turnover rate of 111 percent reported in my best store, a Burger King, was truly a model to emulate. It took almost a year for everyone to quit or be fired there. And I'm not at all surprised that in my worst store, also a Burger King, turnover reached 500 percent. On average, crew members lasted just slightly more than two months—a feat of incredible persistence in my opinion.

To put this into perspective, the majority of companies I have worked with as a consultant over the years report turnover in the 5 percent range for managers and view with alarm any rate over 25 percent for lower-level employees. Why is turnover so much higher in fast food? I blame it on Henry Ford.

Ford had a great idea for building cars: Create jobs that required employees to complete one or two tasks that demanded minimal skills and have those employees repeat those tasks over and over again. In Ford's mind, individual workers were highly interchangeable. If one quit or was fired, another could be hired, trained, and put to work effectively in a matter of hours, if not minutes. I know first-hand: I worked on the Ford Motors' assembly line in Wixom, Michigan, building Lincolns. I started work my first day at 6 a.m. My job was to make 11 spot welds on the car. Someone showed me the welding machine, pointed out the button I pushed to make a "weld," and then showed me where the 11 welds were to be placed on the frame of the car. I watched someone else do my job for 20 minutes, and then I began performing part of the operation by myself, and within two hours I was flying solo. Within two days I was a master of my domain, indistinguishable in skill from the others on my line with years of experience. For a job with this mind-numbing sameness, Henry Ford chose to pay $5 per day, an outrageously princely sum of money in the 1920s. Why so much money—about double the going rate of the day? Nothing about the job was desirable. It was physically demanding, and it was boring. To attract people, he reasoned, he had to pay more than the going rate. And if this added to the price of cars, well, he had very little serious competition at the time.

The people who pioneered fast food revered Ford's

assembly-line methods. They developed operating procedures that were as close to an assembly line as possible. But when it came to imitation, the buck stopped here, quite literally. While Henry had a grand plan to pay handsomely so that his workers could afford the cars they made, fast food had no such goals. Food prices had to be kept significantly lower than the prices in traditional restaurants to attract customers to a completely different business model. Self-serve restaurants with limited menu choices were not the standard in our fathers' (or grandfathers') time. The new fast food restaurants would have to keep labor costs low and standardize operating procedures if they were to keep prices significantly below the typical restaurant of the day. But where Henry "compensated" for unattractive jobs with high wages, fast food developed a two-pronged strategy designed to avoid steep wage costs.

First, they went after a different labor market segment, workers who in the 1950s and 1960s weren't part of the already-existing labor force—teenagers and women with school-aged children. And second, to attract these groups, they offered flexibility. Can't work 9 to 5? No problem. Go to school every day? We'll give you hours after school and on weekends. Kids at school from 8 to 3? No problem. We'll start you at 10 a.m. and let you off at 2 p.m. You can work only summers? Again, no problem. The jump in the applicant pool in the summer offset the drop by parents who took leaves of absence from their fast food jobs when the schools closed for vacations. These attractive hours, combined with efforts to make the job seem more attractive in other dimensions (socialize with others your age, learn skills that will serve you later), were designed to "compensate" for lower wages.

And compensate they do. Fast food stores generally have plenty of applicants, particularly where there is a large teenage population with few other job opportunities. Because of this, fast food stores generally have few problems attracting enough applicants. Keeping them, though, is another thing, and after working in seven stores over 14 months, I think I know the reasons why.

Turnover is sky high because what you see is

not what you get. I was surprised by how hard fast food jobs are. Everything I had seen prepared me for a job that might be repetitive but wouldn't be tiring. After all, watch a Mc-Donald's commercial on television. Everyone is smiling, and there's at least a 50/50 chance someone is going to break into song before the ad is over. Or go into a fast food store, and if you're not greeted with a smile, someone is violating the first commandment of the counter: Thou shalt greet with a smile and make the customer feel welcome!

And should you be at all curious about what the other folks do who make the food that magically appears, well, it's not that easy to discover. Next time you're in a fast food store, try to see how the food is made. Physical barriers, camouflaged as soda dispensers and menu signs and heating trays and holding bins, are all partially intended, I'm convinced, to keep you from seeing what is going on behind the scenes because what you can't see, at least during rush periods, is a pace just this side of frantic: Voices tense with pressure asking for restocking of buns or for more fries to be put in the fry oil to cook; kids literally skating across floors covered with a thin sheen of accumulated grease—this jumble of activity is hidden from view because the dining experience is much more pleasant if customers don't suspect that controlled chaos is the modus operandi.

If you're part of the 70+ percent of customers who get their food from drive-thru, you're even more clueless about what goes on behind the golden arches. All of this serves to camouflage the true nature of fast food jobs. While I will argue that fast food jobs are rewarding, I would never suggest they aren't also very challenging. And the challenge can turn into surprise and then to dismay if you don't enter the application process with at least some sense of the demands placed on fast food workers.

Experts in human resources say it helps cut turnover if you give applicants a realistic preview of what to expect on the job. Hard and dirty? Let them know. Filled with pressure caused by impatient customers watching ticking clocks as short lunch breaks melt away? Only in two jobs did I get advance warning that the job might be more challenging than I expected, and both times it was at a Burger King. The first instance was with a good manager who warned me that things could get very hectic during lunch rush. She also counseled me that the job could be physically demanding, perhaps as much to warn me of what was to come as to see if my "senior" body was prepared for the daily routine. The second instance was less a realistic preview and more a warning. "You don't want to work here," I was warned by the shift supervisor. "It's not a fun place to work." Although the details of why this job was unattractive were sketchy, it was clear from his face that he was serious. No other job gave me even a glimmer of what was forthcoming because, as I mentioned earlier, training isn't realistic.

✳   ✳   ✳

In three of my jobs (Wendy's, both Burger Kings), I spent

my first day watching DVDs that revealed almost none of the on-the-job realities. Every one of the programs pictured a neatly dressed employee, hair perfectly coiffed, wearing a sparkling clean and brand-new uniform. On the real job, in contrast to the images on the training DVD, half the time my uniforms, even the hats, were hand-me-downs from some long-departed crew members. And while I, and the uniforms, started out clean, it didn't take long for the grease to permeate my clothes and my hair. Then there was the pace of the training. Training: slow. Actual job: fast.

The segment on hand washing was typical. The DVD spent 10 minutes working through the complexities of hand washing. It included a test in which I had to estimate the passage of 20 seconds, the amount of time I was expected to lather up and rinse off. If my estimate was wrong, I had to watch the segment again. The segment on sandwich assembly was equally unrealistic. The demonstration takes place in isolation, with only the sound of the crew members' words of instruction interrupting complete silence. You got absolutely no sense of the chaos that percolated in a typical fast food lunch rush from multiple voices shouting instructions, directions, and commands; shrill buzzers announcing the completion of frying cycles; and, in the background, the static-punctuated sounds of drive-thru ordering, which ensured that the cacophony would continue.

Nor was the pace of DVD sandwich assembly anything like the requirements of the real job. Assembling a Quarter Pounder with cheese wasn't inherently hard, but assembling it fast *was*! The DVD conveyed no sense of the urgency created by long lines of impatient customers. The trainer patiently explained where the bun was placed on the wrapper and which items were then placed in what sequence on the bun. Everything was neat and tidy—pickles placed exactly in the center of the bun, spirals of ketchup and mustard flowing in perfect concentric circles. Not a droplet of sweat was anywhere to be seen on the architect of these culinary masterpieces. This idyllic DVD scenario contrasted starkly with the sense of urgency that accompanied an employee's first, and indeed every, lunch rush when he or she was expected to put the *fast* in fast food.

On the other four jobs my training was OJT—on-job training. I watched a trainer who demonstrated the different tasks while explaining each step verbally. Usually these demonstrations were done during slow periods, but with real customers. No simulations: You got to mess up with real people and with real orders. These trainers were like wonderful safety nets, though. When they were there, mistakes seemed small. It was great having someone right behind you to fix your mistakes or to guide you through your own corrective process. This ended, though, with your first solo experience.

If you hadn't quit by this time, soloing could well do the trick. Nothing in the job interview or in the training process prepared you for the anxiety of doing a job you were ill equipped to handle in a time frame guaranteed to promote failure. I can still remember the sinking feeling I had in the early hours of my welding career at Ford when I had completed only 6 or 7 of the 11 welds on those Lincolns as the car frames passed by. That feeling was nothing compared to the anxiety of looking at long lines of impatient customers in a fast food store. At each of the seven fast food jobs I had, I found my first solo to be a very high pressure situation, and I was not alone. It was not at all uncommon to have fast food workers walk off the job on the first day. And when they discovered that lunch rush didn't get all that much easier over time, they left in droves during the first month too. The job just didn't pay enough to tolerate such abuse.

Scientists would say that fast food workers are engaged in "dirty jobs." No, you're not covered in mud when the day is done. Rather, the jobs are ones that people view negatively: funeral parlor employees, garbage collectors, and yes . . . fast food crews.

I remember the first time I experienced this image. Sitting in a booth, catching a quick bite before my shift resumed at my Wendy's job, I was stunned by the way customers behaved around me. It seemed that I was invisible and that it was somehow embarrassing to acknowledge my presence in any way. As I sat, I couldn't help overhearing two women sitting at an adjoining booth less than three feet away, disparaging the dirtiness and general clutter in the dining area—a condition that often resulted from a busy lunch rush. Silently agreeing with them, I vowed to "do the right thing," as the late Dave Thomas had preached. After 10 minutes of diligent cleaning, I approached the two women, who were still sitting and talking, and thanked them for having pointed out the mess that I had just removed. They stared at me blankly, no doubt wondering who I was and how I had divined their conversation. When I explained that I had been sitting next to them and had accidentally overheard their conversation, I was greeted again with a look of incomprehension. I don't believe I appeared on their radar screen at all. It's an eerie—and degrading—feeling to be so invisible.

Not appearing on the radar screen, though, may well have been what many crew members wished for. At one of my jobs my biggest hurdle to being hired was convincing the manager that I wouldn't be like all the other "school teachers" she had hired in the past who would quit after being recognized by customers who were also these teachers' students. I've seen crew members attempt to hide evidence of their employment by wearing jackets on warm days or carrying their hats buried in their hands. Both were gestures designed, I suspect, to hide the "demeaning truth."

Piled on top of the job's surprisingly challenging demands and low prestige, there was a remarkable lack of early feedback and encouragement from managers to offset these negatives. I wished someone had whispered to me, "Hey, it gets

FROM BEHIND THE COUNTER

Who's got the dirtiest job? I often wondered. On my second day at Arby's, a kid from the car wash two doors down the street comes in for his lunch break. Guessing that I am new, he tells me bitterly how he was fired by Arby's for not showing up on a day he claimed he wasn't scheduled (this is probably why Don has us sign the schedule sheet, as proof that we have seen it). The kid also proudly notes that he has just been selected Employee of the Month at the car wash. What does this indicate? Is a job at the car wash better than a job at Arby's? I wonder what their turnover rate is!

easier, hang in there." Or simply offered a word of encouragement like "You're doing very well for the first day." While a couple of my managers understood the value of a well-timed compliment, most acted as though praise was a priceless commodity. I suspected that many fast food workers were starved for a little recognition, and when none came in these jobs, they left for other, more supportive environments.

Fast food turnover statistics included people who were fired, and one of the biggest reasons for termination was theft. One of my managers noted that in the 15 months he had worked as manager, he had fired about one employee a month. Of these terminations, 10 were for theft. One of the cases was major, with more than $3,000 missing from the till in an elaborate doctoring of the books by an assistant manager. Other employees were dismissed because they left at night with big bags of food or supplies or because they were discovered giving discounts or free food to friends. The remaining five crew members were fired for poor performance. Admittedly, he acknowledged, firing for poor performance was rare. "I moved people to other jobs when they just didn't get it, hoping I could find a job that fit their skills. Usually this worked."

Turnover isn't necessarily a bad thing. At low levels,

it often serves to bring new blood into a company, and this infusion can bring new ideas and ward off complacency. But at some point turnover becomes costly. Every good management book documents these standard costs (for example, the expense of filling the empty position, the lost knowledge and contacts of the departed employee, and the lost productivity while training a new employee). Most experts don't acknowledge, though, the debilitating impact of persistently high turnover—turnover at the levels common in most fast food stores. There is a cultural impact of turnover that's not unlike the "army brat" phenomenon: When parents are frequently transferred from base to base, their kids can become isolated and withdrawn. Making friends isn't productive because the next move is just around the corner. I've seen the same thing in fast food stores with high turnover.

In every store I worked, there was a stable core of long-timers. Let's say they accounted for 10 employees out of a staff of 30. To get 200 percent turnover, the 20 short-timers would have to have left, on average, three times per year. Now think about this: You're part of the stable group. Any new person hired has a likelihood of being gone in four months. Are you likely to invest time in building a relationship? The answer is probably no. And this tends to further aggravate the situation. In five of my seven jobs, there was an invisible yet palpable social barrier. On one side was the core group, with their own inside jokes and rules of the game. On the other side were the newcomers, frustrated by the job and by the separatism. In my least favorite job, the 500 percent turnover reality reinforced a culture in which none of the core group even bothered to acknowledge new crew members. Why bother even learning my name? Chances were I wouldn't be there long enough to make the effort worthwhile. And I must admit, this isolation contributed to my dislike of the job. When I left, I actually felt relief for the only time in my seven-job odyssey.

Fast food jobs taught me some invaluable lessons about reducing turnover. The easiest-to-implement lessons: People don't like bad surprises, so take the time to explain what's going to happen if it's apt to be negative. Most of us like predictability, at least in our jobs—tell me what to expect over the long run. Of course, such descriptions are broad strokes, and they may be wrong, but at least I've been exposed to the future. Conversely, telling me "you'll find this job easy" and then exposing me to a job that isn't . . . well, that is just begging me to find some way to get out. Asking me to do something I don't have the skill set to accomplish also is a bad surprise. In most of my fast food jobs, I had no idea what was coming up in the first days of the job. Even when I was a seasoned veteran—by my fourth job I had at least a general idea of the job's demands—I still was nervous and ill prepared for the specific tasks in new settings.

The personalities of the people you work with can also make or break a job. Managers I know seem to think that the way to create a good social fit is a mystery. I don't agree. Hiring people with common interests helps. Selection interviews aren't just about identifying those people with a good work ethic. They are also about identifying those individuals with enough similarities to others in the existing group to encourage friendship to percolate.

Good managers select for fit. Will the applicant fit in with the current crew? I use a bit of sarcasm in my communications. My best manager discovered this in the interview. She admitted that my tendency to be sarcastic was a big part of why I was hired—the rest of the crew loved to banter, and sarcasm was the social currency. To select "for fit" means understanding the crew's collective personality. Kris at Burger King organized after-work social functions. Yes, they were intended to build friendships among the crew members. But Kris also got a chance to see how the group interacted— what worked and didn't work in forming bonds. I think this knowledge helped Kris hire people who would complement each other and—more importantly—stay in the job.

Reflections
on Fast Food

I'm back at my regular job now, teaching graduate-level business students about people in jobs and the human resources practices that affect them. Many of my latest examples of how people are hired, trained, and rewarded come from my days in fast food restaurants. Students find the stories entertaining and, I hope, informative. I want the students to be good managers, and I think examples from fast food will help. Yesterday evening, though, I got an e-mail from one of my former students that caused me to think. A Korean man, he explained in awkward English that he had worked seven years in Korea as a corporate trainer for McDonald's, and then he added what to him appeared perfectly obvious: "You seem not to like fast food."

I am troubled by this observation. Is all that I teach about fast food negative? By extension, does this mean that I think there is nothing in the fast food world worth teaching about managing employees that would help managers in other industries? Quite the contrary. In fact, as I was thinking about these questions, I opened USA Today to see in the article "Would You Like Life Skills with That Burger Job?" that McDonald's is starting a new ad campaign focusing on how burger jobs help their employees build life skills, including how to lead people. Working in fast food gives people many life skills that they can use productively elsewhere. I would go even further and say that I've had plenty of reasons in the past 14 months to agree with this sentence: "I look for people with fast food on their résumé."

I was recently at a cocktail party speaking with an executive for a big pharmaceutical company when we got to talking about my fast food experiences—a topic that seems to fascinate the people I come into contact with. Spontaneously, he mentioned that he looks for people who have worked in fast food. Even though his misspent youth took him in other directions, he had found that people who have held jobs in the fast food industry have three indispensable qualities: They know how to do what the job requires, they get it done when it needs to be done, and they aren't afraid of hard work and pressure.

Most of us see fast food jobs from a very one-sided view: We walk in during lunch rush when everyone behind the counter is working at breakneck speed, and through this lens we see a lot of negatives. The pay isn't very good. How do we know? There's a sign perpetually plastered on the window: "Now Hiring—Up to $6.75 Starting." We can also see that the job is hard. Certainly working in a retail store in the local mall pays at least as well and is far less arduous. And the customer in front of the fast food counter is always right.

If I think long enough about the day-to-day grind of fast food, many of the memories that emerge are negative. Often I was treated like a cog that was interchangeable with any of the 200 applicants waiting to be hired. My opinion seemed not to matter. My role was clearly defined, and I knew exactly what I was supposed to do, which more often than not was to operate under extreme time pressures. And when

I was done, there was rarely an "atta boy." I looked down at my uniform and there were stray droplets of mustard intermingled with grease. The secondhand hat I had to wear was soaked with perspiration, mine intermingled with past generations of fast food workers. These short-term reflections suggest the job was hardly worth it. Certainly when my observations are colored by three herniated discs earned on the McJob, the experience wasn't positive.

But six months later, my back on the mend, I'm more inclined to agree with that pharmaceutical executive. The people I met in fast food weren't afraid to work, and they took pride in doing a job well that most people don't appreciate or, for that matter, think about at all. I'm reminded of the words uttered by one of my Ph.D.'ed colleagues as we shared an elevator ride up to our respective offices, "I can't imagine anyone else in the school taking on a research project like this." I'm sure he meant this statement to reinforce an image I like to perpetuate—crazy professor willing to do anything that catches his fancy, even work in a job with so little social status. But my first reaction, which I did not share with him because I doubt he would have understood, was one of pride. Pride at having worked fast food, for however briefly, and having never let the job beat me down. Pride at having been told (occasionally) I was doing a good job. Working with kids one-third my age, I not only survived serious pressure and endless physical tasks, I even came to be accepted as someone who could be counted on when the burgers were flying and the orders were backlogging. Where my well-meaning colleague saw an offbeat professor tilting at windmills, I saw someone who had emerged better for the experience. The same can be said of kids who may not realize right away what a job in fast food means but who will emerge better for the experience in later years.

* * *

The hard currency of fast food is reliability. If you aren't

reliable, you will be weeded out quickly. At home you may be able to get away with saying "I'll do it tomorrow" or "Give me 15 minutes, Mom." In fast food, though, you better show up on the day you're told and at the time you're told. Show up early, and you can't clock in until it's time. Don't show up, and you better have a fantastic excuse. Don't show up a second time, and don't bother with an excuse—you'll have all the free time you want. It's hard to object to this reality because everyone working around you accepts it. Further, you experience firsthand the costs when someone doesn't show up.

Someone doesn't show, someone else quits, on top of two people short already: This is a common occurrence in fast food. Managers staff lean. If they can survive lunch rush with the minimum, the rest of the shift is easily handled. But if something goes wrong, and it frequently does, crew members are scrambling to keep up with the lines. Reliable crew members are vital.

FROM BEHIND THE COUNTER

All hell breaks loose today. Amber doesn't show. Someone named Karen quits (no explanation is given by anyone when this is announced), and apparently we are already two people short. This leaves a total of seven. They put Bret on sandwiches. He's a great utility man because that job allows him to get cigarette breaks when he wants and to go at his own pace. Unlike utility, the assembly jobs are the focal point of stress during lunch rush. When the pace and stress rise, Bret loses control quickly. At the height of rush, he makes two chicken sandwiches wrong and throws them to the floor in anger. The computer screen doesn't forgive, though, so he quickly goes back to the job.

You are bombarded with feedback in fast food. And even though I didn't realize it at the time, the environment is perfect for teaching kids the art of giving and receiving feedback. Every job has specific guidelines for how to do it.

Fast food workers learn almost by osmosis the importance of telling workers what is expected of them. Make a mistake during rush and it throws everything and everyone off. One day I forgot to check the supply of Angus Burgers. It was midrush, and Daniel yelled back, "I need Angus." By the time I got them out of the freezer, fed them into the broiler,

> Thomas (owner's son) helps again but leaves early. I am managing to keep up with the buns and broiler, but because we are short-handed, I try new territories, occasionally cooking fries and getting supplies for the front. As it turns out, I am not ready for this self-initiated jump, and I get behind on everything. When Jeff comes on shift, he is angry that I have let the inventory of burgers fall below accepted levels. I testily tell him we are just trying to survive here short-handed. In the middle of all this, Bret lets the stress of being understaffed get him again—he announces to me in an easily overheard tone that he doesn't like Tammy because apparently she "rests" in the middle of the aisles rather than standing to the side. Clearly this is a comment on Tammy's weight, which probably tops out over 250. I must remember these are just kids.

and got the cooked versions to Daniel, he was not only out of Angus but also low on everything else I neglected while rushing for Angus. I never caught up, which is why deviations from expectations are met with immediate feedback.

Feedback is a fast food reality. Don't do something right, don't do something fast enough, and you're told what's wrong and how to fix it. The feedback is always about performance.

You also learn how to give feedback, something I teach in my classes and a lesson Angie has learned to perfection working fast food. Everyone in fast food pays attention to new workers, at least in terms of performance. We need to

FROM BEHIND THE COUNTER

One of the assistant managers tells Tammy she's getting behind on first assembly board. Lunch rush is just building, and she needs to do better at directing the sandwich assembly of the girl on second board. There's only one computer screen, so first board must direct the efforts of second board. Between them they must make all the nonspecial sandwiches. Very quickly, though, it's apparent we will never speed up with Tammy at first board. The assistant manager motions for Angie to come take Tammy's place, and Tammy is moved to the specials board. It's Friday, and mostly fish sandwiches are coming up on the specials screen, and they're relatively easy to make. Tammy has been treated no differently than any other worker.

learn jobs quickly, and we're thrown into dozens of new procedures. When we forget or make a mistake, someone is there to correct. It's expected, and it's part of every fast food culture I worked in. You quickly learn two important lessons in leadership:

1. Be as specific as possible when telling new people their jobs.

2. Then make sure you or someone else follows their progress and corrects behaviors before they become bad habits.

Some managers even cover a third key aspect of giving feed-back—explain why the change in behavior is important.

* * *

I would argue that there aren't many jobs—at any wage

rate—with more daily pressure than fast food. Every day at lunchtime the capacities of equipment and crew are tested by lines of customers that seem only to get longer at an accelerating rate. Part of the strain is inflicted by managers ever conscious of the labor dollars they are spending. Many states won't let employers schedule workers for shifts shorter than 3 hours, so a manager who staffs to adequately cover a 1.5-hour lunch rush also has to pay all those crew members when the rush is over. It tears at their hearts—and wallets—to do this since bonuses are often linked to cutting labor costs.

More often than not, managers intentionally understaff at lunch. I can recall only three days when we didn't face intense pressure to get food out quickly at lunchtime. One day in a Buffalo Arby's, there was a snowstorm. My manager fretted the whole time we were there. Once clocked in, the law stated we had to be paid for three hours. The other two times were at a Wendy's adjacent to a McDonald's. Wednesday was 49-cent Cheeseburger Day at MickeyD's. Need I say more?

Too few people filling too many orders; managers urging us to pick up the speed; timers going off, indicating something in the deep fryer needing immediate attention; team members loudly yelling for some kind of assistance: more something, faster something, fill something, get something, change something! We were all affected by the barrage of

FROM BEHIND THE COUNTER

We have no assistant manager here, James says, to save on the labor bill. He's judged on his labor costs, and bonuses depend on his keeping them low. It comes back to haunt him, though, when someone needs an unexpected day off. Apparently this is why *he* frequently ends up with 16- to 24-hour shifts.

cues, but we also knew that sooner or later, it would end. And when it ended, no one celebrated a victory. Pressure came every day; pressure was met every day. By its being accepted without special recognition, pressure was relegated to the ordinary—to be met, to be dealt with, and to be forgotten when it passed. How many 21-year-olds are field tested and certified ready like that? A certain quiet confidence germinates, surfacing in the inevitable pressures of later jobs, much to the delight of unsuspecting managers. It's no wonder that the pharmaceutical executive I talked to actually looks for people with this kind of experience under their belts!

Few jobs demand interdependence like fast foods. You

can't survive without the help of others. If I don't toast buns quickly enough, sandwich assemblers are left waiting. If Janie gets behind on fries, orders begin to stack up. Fill an order too slowly, and whoever is working front register is blistered

FROM BEHIND THE COUNTER

I'm having trouble getting the heavy boxes of frozen patties into the short-term-storage freezer. Once I pull the plastic sack out of the cardboard box, gravity immediately shifts the burgers to the bottom. The resulting teardrop shape is unwieldy and difficult to get into the small opening made by the sliding door of the freezer. Seeing me struggle, Bret comes over and pulls the freezer out from its snug cubbyhole. Then he pulls the whole sliding door off its track and places it to the side. Now I lower the patties into the freezer with ease. Bret follows almost immediately by reinserting the freezer door and sliding the whole freezer back to its original position. As he leaves, he acknowledges he learned the trick from someone else, and under similar circumstances.

by angry customers. A team member unexpectedly doesn't show up one day and everyone pays a price. Two don't show up, and chaos reigns.

It's impossible not to build team skills. Communication isn't a luxury; it's a necessity. If I yell out that I need someone to get me Whopper patties from the freezer, I'm confident someone will acknowledge and assist. If I'm having trouble with a task, someone steps up to help.

It is almost a sacred truth in human resources circles that it's easier to train people in technical skills than in interpersonal skills. I think fast food's strength is that it's a crucible for identifying and building the interpersonal skills that matter. I don't think anyone would claim that fast foods build technical skills that enhance marketability, but if you get hired into fast foods and you survive the job, you emerge with interpersonal talents that will serve you well later in life.

Big old guys don't usually work the front counter.

Everything in fast food is designed to make customers feel comfortable. Menus are generally the same across the country; store interiors look pretty much the same; and the person working the front counter is chosen for affability. In my experience, front counter jobs went to polite people, usually women. Guys and the more roughly hewn women worked in the back. Only twice did I get thrown into this position— once at Arby's and once at my second McDonald's job. Besides having to decipher the hieroglyphics of the computer-register, I had to be a goodwill ambassador. Although no one ever gave me a script to follow in interactions with customers (in contrast to what some books on the industry have suggested is common practice), on both jobs I was told how to handle irate customers—refer them to the manager.

Watching managers deal with angry customers was a study in classic conflict management, right out of the textbooks we use at school. Find out the problem; let the customer vent; listen attentively; ask for clarification; find out what the customer expects to resolve the conflict; if it's reasonable, fill the request as quickly as possible, apologizing again and thanking the customer for his or her business; if the request isn't reasonable, make an alternative suggestion, always trying to defuse anger and maintain a positive attitude. I witnessed several of these exchanges, and so did other crew members. It wasn't hard to notice angry customers, and many of us were curious about the problem and its resolution, as long as we didn't have to be part of the "bomb crew" defusing it.

The bigger problems were the difficult customers who flew under the "anger radar"—that is, they were angry but not angry enough to warrant our summoning the manager. Those we usually had to deal with ourselves. It wasn't acceptable for us to get angry and risk escalation, so more often than not, we simply filled the order as quickly as possible and rejoiced internally as they walked away. Two lessons that serve well in life are to be learned in fast food: Stay task-oriented and know that the unpleasantness will end.

Learning to cope is an invaluable life and work skill, and if there's anything you learn in fast food, it's how to cope. In fact, the skills learned in fast food are like a great wine: The richness of the reward isn't evident at first, but it can truly grow with time.

* * *

And what about that "condom" that started this whole

adventure? I certainly understand now why the store manager responded to me by trying to defuse the situation—he was playing by the book, as was the district manager who offered me a month of free sandwiches. How did that piece of sanitary glove end up on my daughter's sandwich in the first place? I still have no clue whatsoever. But I wouldn't trade all the insight I gained on the McJob for anything in the world. Except maybe a Whopper. Hold the lettuce!

Index

Note: Italic *f* indicates material in a footnote.

About the Author

JERRY M. NEWMAN, PH.D., is a University Distinguished
Teaching Professor for the State University of New York at
Buffalo. He is the coauthor of *Compensation*, which has
been the bestselling book in the category for 21 years. He is
also an advisor to firms including AT&T, Hewlett-Packard,
Burger King, McDonald's, and Nabisco.